Dangerous
Sea
Creatures

Dangerous
Sea
Creatures

A COMPLETE GUIDE
TO HAZARDOUS MARINE LIFE

by Thomas Helm

FUNK & WAGNALLS
New York

Photo credits appear on page 270.

To my wife, Dorothy

Contents

Dangerous
Sea
Creatures

Seascape.

1

Introduction

The sea is so vast and its inhabitants so varied and numerous as to resemble another world within our world. It has always drawn man toward it with a magnetic attraction, forever beckoning, yet steadfastly resisting thorough exploration and complete comprehension. Thus it has been from mankind's beginning and will continue until the end of time, for it is doubtful that the sea will ever reveal all of its secrets.

The accumulation of knowledge concerning this other world has increased more in this century than in the preceding thousands of years, but in many respects the exploration has just begun. Technological advances developed even within the past few decades have provided better means of investigation than were ever thought possible. Theories and scientific beliefs, long held inviolate, have had to be revised and some have vanished like soap bubbles. Yet, it seems that for each riddle satisfactorily solved, another is discovered, and often the new problem is more perplexing than the one it replaced.

Man has learned, by injury and sometimes by witnessing violent death, that some of the sea's inhabitants are hostile toward him. Frequently his fears are a combination of imagination and fragments of folklore not far removed from the age of mythology. He knows, however, that the sea is an alien world that resists conquest and because of this it represents a region of mystery. For that matter, anything man contacts and cannot fully understand constitutes a mystery and often becomes fraught with doubt and apprehension and even fear.

One need only approach a dark alley between rows of buildings and immediately the conscious mind is prodded with an instinct as old as the human race. Quite likely the alley contains nothing more than an assortment of rubbish cans and perhaps a stray cat out on a nightly prowl. But, because the human vision cannot penetrate the gloom, man suspects it may harbor some form of danger. As he draws nearer he wonders if some villain, waiting to inflict violent harm, is lurking in the shadows.

Again, the scene may be some lonely road that winds its way through unfamiliar territory. In the light of day it would likely be viewed as a pleasant bucolic landscape. In the black of night, however, the traveler cannot see what flanks the road and hopes he will not be forced to stop in this unknown region.

When man began his tenure on earth it probably was not long before he wandered down to the beach and looked out across the vast expanse of the sea. Just to speculate on what his reactions must have been fires the imagination. If he saw it first on a sunlit day the sparkling surface must have appeared inviting. Almost certainly he was awed at the size, realizing that it stretched away far beyond the limit of his vision. In all probability it was only a matter of minutes before he encountered his first disappointment. The sight of so much water likely aroused his thirst, but that which he took into his mouth was decidedly different from the water of lakes and streams.

Spitting and gagging he withdrew in haste, wondering if the briny water was some form of poison. This discovery alone probably caused him considerable concern, for if he could not drink it neither could the deer, nor the bear, nor the rabbit, nor any of the other creatures he depended upon for food. Just that first taste may have filled him with fear that caused him to turn and run away.

Whether he ran or stayed is of little importance, because it is certain that sooner or later he, or someone like him, returned to further ponder this vast mystery. Quite probably he soon spotted a fish or schools of them swimming close to shore. He had already learned that fish from other waters provided him with food. He had developed some skill in capturing them with spears, clubs, or crudely woven nets, and it was undoubtedly a pleasant surprise to discover that those first fish he sampled were not briny like the water from which they had been taken.

Gathering fish for food was undoubtedly an attraction, but it was more than fish that whetted his curiosity about this strange new world. On land he could see, touch, hear, and smell the things around him. He could do much the same in the very shallow water close to shore, but when he swam or floated on a log out over deeper water, everything was quite different.

From the surface all he could do was look down with hazy vision and wonder what kind of world existed below. Now and then he would see strange creatures, unlike fish and vastly different from the land animals. Some seemed to fly and glide like birds, but they did not resemble the birds he knew. Some creatures crawled, slithered, or plodded across the almost obscure bottom. In the void between bottom and surface there were those that flashed by almost too swiftly to be seen. Occasionally, creatures of great size leaped clear of the surface, landing with a loud splash that sent up showers of spray. Others simply broke the surface with strange sounds, vanishing swiftly back into the gloomy depths.

When he waded about in the shallows he found most of the strange forms of life he could catch provided him with food, but he also discovered others were dangerous to touch. Some stung him, causing either mild or severe pain, and once in a while he watched a companion die after being bitten or stung. He also learned that certain creatures made him ill if he ate them. One day, as he stood on the beach and watched, he saw a large fish cruise into the shallow water. It moved near a fellow human who was ducking below to collect shellfish. Suddenly this man thrashed the water with his arms and screamed for help, but the great fish pulled him out to deeper water and the victim was gone before anyone could decide how to help him.

Day by day, year by year, man came to the conclusion that the sea was much like the forest and jungle. It offered him many forms of food, but there was always the chance that some creature was waiting to hurt or kill him. On land, however, he could build a fire to keep the lion or bear away. If something chased him he could run or climb a tree for safety. If there was a venomous snake in his path he could walk around it or smash it with his club. But, even waist-deep in the sea it was quite different. The drag of the water prevented him from running, it was difficult to see where he was putting his feet, and, much to his dismay, some of the creatures were not frightened by his angry shouts and paid little or no heed to his weapons.

Still, even the earliest humans must have found it was pleasant to splash about in the clean salt water. It washed them, and when they came out they felt refreshed. It was also comfortable to rest on the soft sand while the sun warmed their bodies. Thus not only did the sea provide them with an abundance of food but it afforded them pleasure. Also, there was still another less tangible force that drew them down to the beach. There was something about this strangely different world that whetted their imagination.

Dawn man found that he needed to be entertained when his day's work was done and before it was time to fall asleep. No doubt various forms of dancing and attempts to make music occupied him to some extent. As his vocabulary increased and his ability to converse with others widened, he learned that telling and listening to stories was a form of entertainment that required no ceremonial preparation. Logically, the favorite raconteurs were the ones who could hold the attention of the listeners with the most exciting tales.

Because no one knew how many yet unseen creatures lived in the sea, the yarn spinner with the most active imagination had an unlimited source of material. All that was necessary was to inject a smattering of truth, such as identifying some creature the others had seen. For example, they had occasionally watched a school of giant mantas leaping and somersaulting in a nearby bay. Their size and fearsome countenance was all the tale-teller needed.

Those who listened began tossing more logs on the fire and gripping their spears more tightly when they heard how certain of these batlike monsters left the sea at night and soared about over the countryside, capturing humans and descending with them into the dark recesses of some subterranean cave. Again, on some distant stretch of the coast, there was an octopus—a hundred times larger than the little ones they had seen. As the story unfolded they shuddered to learn that this dreadful beast would slither up the hillside and make off with half the members of a tribe clutched in its eight enormous sucker-studded arms.

Fanciful tales of strange and dangerous sea creatures were not restricted to early man. Even with the passage of aeons, when many languages had been perfected and the written word was there to be read by countless people who had never seen the great waters, the sea still remained a region of mystery. Not only had it been found to cover a far larger area than early man could imagine but men had sailed far out onto it, bringing back stories of monsters and demons that were a constant threat to the sailors and their ships. Who was there to dispute them? Those who lived close to the sea but never ventured far out on it had seen many incredible forms of sea life even in the shallows. It was therefore entirely plausible that the farther out one went, the greater and more numerous the dangerous creatures were sure to be.

In the course of man's struggle to better understand his world, a select group, to be known as marine scientists, began the almost Sisyphean task of making some kind of order out of the chaotic mystery that involved the sea and its inhabitants. One of the outstanding leaders of this group was Aristotle. In his lifetime he covered such a wide spectrum of science in general as to be almost inconceivable. Without even a microscope to aid him, he contributed so much useful knowledge about sea life that many of his observations still stand as a guideline of study.

The history of scientific study of sea creatures is

punctuated with established facts that have been later disproven and seemingly farfetched fables that eventually have been discovered to be accurate. Between these two extremes, there always exists a gray zone of beliefs that may or may not be true. The eminent naturalist and physician Rondelet (1507–1566) has often been cited as an example of someone who wore the cloak of intelligence, only to be unable to resist publishing an occasional fanciful tale.

He was apparently fascinated with the danger of the dreaded dogfish (shark) and reported observing one chasing a man along the beach. Impossible! Utterly ridiculous! Or is it? The answer to an all-important question is lost in the backwash of time. Before completely discrediting Rondelet, it would be of interest to know just exactly what he meant in referring to the beach. If his use of the word meant up on the dry sand, then he deserves the frequent criticism accorded him. But, there is the distinct possibility that he actually did observe a man running in the shallow water. This area is also known as the beach and if this is what Rondelet meant, it puts an entirely different light on the picture. Sharks have been known to literally ground themselves when in hot pursuit of their prey.

A fact that should never be overlooked is that no branch of science is complete, nor will it ever be as long as mankind is interested in a subject and wonders why it cannot be more fully explained. Regrettably, there are always a few who have conducted extensive investigation and feel no one should dispute their word. In adopting such an attitude they have ceased to function as scientists, because it is almost certain that sooner or later new evidence will be introduced that will, in some measure, change the original findings.

One of the most outstanding examples of how "established facts" can be dashed to pieces practically overnight concerns the depth at which life in the sea can exist. After centuries of detailed and carefully assembled facts, it was concluded that life stopped at a depth of about half a mile. It was not just the word of one scientist, but the collective thinking of many sagacious students of marine biology.

Many related facts were accumulated and carefully

examined before the conclusion was reached: The pressure was unquestionably too great, the water was too cold, and the light from the sun could not penetrate such depths. All were perfectly reasonable assumptions, but man had yet to learn that the sea does not necessarily abide by what is considered logic.

Oddly enough, when Samuel Morse invented the telegraph in 1837 he had set the stage for some revolutionary thinking in the field of marine biology. Later, in 1858, Cyrus W. Field laid a telegraph cable across the Atlantic Ocean. It is quite likely that Field, knowledgeable as he was about engineering, electronics, and oceanography, was more than mildly interested in the creatures of the sea. It was only when his cable eventually broke and had to be hauled to the surface for repairs that the college of marine science was shaken to its strongest foundations.

If the break had occurred in water less than half a mile in depth, it probably would have gone virtually unnoticed by any save those who depended upon it for swift communication. Instead, the two ends had to be lifted from far greater depths and when it was up in the light of day, it was discovered that forms of sea life had affixed themselves to it. It is likely some of the standpatters in the field of marine biology could not have been more overwhelmed if someone had captured a fire-breathing sea monster straight out of the pages of mythology and hemmed it up in a cove for any and all to see.

Field's broken telegraph cable signaled the twilight for the old guard of marine biology. Among those who subscribed to the established depth range of sea life was an outstanding marine scientist by the name of Dr. Edward Forbes. He, like so many of his colleagues, found the discovery difficult to accept. Dr. Forbes, however, was more flexible in his thinking and he was willing to agree that he, his contemporaries, and predecessors had erred in their calculations. Instead of grousing and mumbling and attempting to find some error in the proof on the cable, Dr. Forbes said, in effect, "If we have been this wrong for so long, who can say what other mistakes we are teaching?"

It was largely through his efforts that an even larger door was opened to marine science. At his insistence, H.M.S. *Challenger* was commissioned in 1872 to set forth on a three-year voyage around the world. This fact-finding voyage of the *Challenger* was destined to make even more startling discoveries concerning the sea and its inhabitants.

For countless thousands of years those interested in unraveling the mysteries of the sea had to be content to observe the surface and attempt to form conclusions. Their only assistance came from reports of skin divers who went down in shallow water to gather sponges and pearl oysters. Additional help came from fishermen who often hauled some previously unknown creature to the surface and, of course, bits and pieces of strange creatures occasionally washed ashore. A giant step was taken when the helmeted diver could go deeper and stay longer, but even then, he was severely restricted by depth and the length of his air hose.

It can hardly be disputed that the twentieth century was well advanced before really significant strides were taken in the gathering of valuable data about the sea. With the steadily increasing development of electronic equipment it is now possible to actually see the bottom at depths far greater than any diver could be expected to descend. Other equipment can give highly accurate topographical readings that have been of inestimable value to submarine transportation.

It is almost certain that the deepest valley anywhere on earth has been located. It is in the western Pacific and known as the Mariana Trench, exceeding 36,000 feet in depth. If Mount Everest, with its peak slightly over 29,000 feet, could be dropped into this basement of the world it would be covered by over a mile of water.

On January 23, 1960, Jacques Piccard and U.S. Navy Lieutenant Don Walsh descended into this abyss to a depth of 35,800 feet in the bathyscaphe *Trieste*. Their stay on the bottom was limited to twenty minutes, but in this brief period, with the aid of a powerful floodlight, they spotted a fish making its way across the bottom ooze. It was not some strange monster of weird proportions, but rather a flatfish about a foot long and not unlike the common flounder or sole found in the shallow water close to shore.

Just to consider this sighting of a living fish swimming in a region of absolute darkness, intense cold, and where the pressure is measured in vast numbers of tons per square inch is of decided interest. Especially so when it is recalled that such a relatively short time ago the best scientific minds were convinced that no life could exist beyond a depth of half a mile.

Despite the enormous contributions to science, it is doubtful that the heroic dive by Walsh and Piccard can compare to the development of the Aqualung. Jacques-Yves Cousteau, Frédéric Dumas, and those who worked with them during and after World War II opened an entirely different route of exploration into the sea.

Here, for the first time, was a dependable piece of equipment that allowed the scientist and interested layman to descend at a leisurely pace far down into shoal waters. The design of scuba is so well perfected that a human can carry a dependable supply of air far deeper than is generally needed, or even wanted. With its advent, an important dimension was added to the study of the abundant and varied forms of sea life that are most frequently contacted by the average person.

There is considerable difference in dissecting and studying the preserved body of a creature on the laboratory table and the opportunity of closely observing that same creature while it is still alive in its natural element. This in no manner means the laboratory scientist is outdated. Instead, he has been offered an extra hand to aid him in his work. It has, in fact, become almost standard practice for the professional marine biologist to become proficient in scuba diving, so that he may better understand what he later subjects to detailed analysis on the table.

The diver, whether scientist or layman, can drop into the water and watch as different fish go about their feeding. He can follow a stingray and note the method it employs to cover its body with sand or mud to escape detection from its enemies. By suspending himself with natural buoyancy he can safely observe the trailing tentacles of a Portuguese man-of-war as it paralyzes a shrimp or small fish and draws it up to its mouth.

Prior to the effortless scuba diving, the observer had only the choice of making hurried surface dives, with his stay underwater limited by the length of time he could comfortably hold his breath. Alternatively, he could dress himself in the cumbersome habiliments of the helmeted diver and enlist the aid of several other persons to handle the air pumps, lifelines, air hose, and related impedimenta to assure his safety underwater.

Drifting about at a chosen depth, the scuba diver can become a part of the underwater environment. Without distracting the quiet calm of the undersea world he can gain a far more comprehensive picture of how both harmless and dangerous creatures cohabit in the same area under normal conditions. Occasionally, a fairly accurate observation can be made through the glass walls of an aquarium, but, at best, it only suggests how the subject reacts when not confined and free to move about as it chooses.

Despite the vast array of equipment that enables modern man to explore the undersea world, no one has yet been able to overcome the problem of suitable light for proper investigation. Even in seemingly clear water a gloomy darkness is often encountered at a depth of a hundred feet. As the diver descends the natural light fades swiftly, blocked by suspended particles of plankton and sediments. If this load is heavy in the water the amount of usable light may be absent at depths as shallow as twenty-five feet.

Artificial light is of unquestionable value, but it often causes many forms of sea life to react in an unnatural manner. Some are fascinated and will be drawn toward it as insects are drawn toward a light on a dark night. However interesting this may be to the diver who is down only to see the sights, it is not what the serious observer wants. Once a creature is distracted, even though it may not be frightened, its normal behavior is interrupted.

It is fortunate, however, that most of the sea creatures the

Scuba diver.

average swimmer and casual skin diver are most interested in observing are found in the zone that is sufficiently illuminated by daylight. It is true that many of them frequently move from very shallow water to great depths, but investigating them in water where they can clearly be seen is far better than only guessing at what takes place on the bottom.

For countless centuries those who have written about the creatures of the sea were divided into two fundamental groups. One has been the fiction writer who, while he may provide excellent entertainment, is primarily concerned with constructing a yarn—often with little regard for the truth. The other has been the dedicated scientist who knows what he is writing about, but in order to establish his point so it will be satisfactory to fellow scientists, has a habit of cloaking his knowledge in esoteric terms that confuse the average reader.

In the fairly recent past a new form of writer appeared on the scene and has come to be known as the debunker. His practice is to take an established fact and make it seem that new evidence has been uncovered that disproves that which is believed. As a rule, to accomplish this, the debunker chooses one-sided selections—often taken out of context—and stresses these points. If he is skilled at his trade, he can make his story quite plausible, especially to those who are seeking the truth but cannot become sufficiently involved to make their own investigation and form their own opinions.

Regrettably, such debunking often comes from the pen of writers who have established their names as ones who can be depended upon for accurate reporting. In recent years the shark has been one of the subjects that has attracted the attention of these writers. The general theme is to prove beyond a shadow of a doubt that the shark is as timid as a cottontail rabbit, or some similar nonsense. Either omitted or skimmed over lightly are the countless cases of proven attacks, concentrating instead on the numerous times sharks will turn tail and swim away.

There can be little doubt that the potential danger of many sea creatures has been grossly overrated. Nevertheless, one cannot help but wonder if the debunker is not just as guilty of misrepresenting facts as the fiction writer who suggests there is a ravenous monster lurking in every cove.

Caught in the middle is the occasional visitor to the sea-coast. Today, his store of knowledge is far broader than was that of his predecessors a few generations ago. Even if his interest in sea life is only mediocre, it is almost certain that he has been exposed to an abundance of newspaper and magazine articles, as well as television and motion picture documentaries. In contrast to his grandparents, he has literally been surfeited with an overabundance of information.

This occasional visitor might be well versed on the fauna of his native region. Therefore, he reasonably assumes that when he reaches the coast he can depend on local inhabitants to accurately answer any normal question he may ask about sea creatures. It may *seem* a logical conclusion, but it is one that all too often is far removed from fact. Just because a person happens to live close to the sea is no guarantee that he knows much about it. Often his knowledge is more distorted than some who live a thousand miles away from salt water.

Recently, while tightening the lines on our boat after returning to the local marina, we could not help overhearing an interesting conversation between two men who had strolled out on the nearest catwalk. The accents of the two quickly disclosed that one was a native and the other was midwestern. The conversation was as follows:

VISITOR: This surely is a beautiful part of the country. Do you live around here?

LOCAL: Been here all my life, except for a couple of years in Europe when I was in the army.

VISITOR: Well, maybe you can answer a question for me. The wife and I were out at the beach early this morning and we were watching some big fish that looked like the one in that television show. Seems some call them dolphins and others call them porpoise, but that's beside the point. They have to breathe air like regular animals, don't they?

LOCAL: Sure do. Sometimes if you happen to be close by and there isn't too much noise you can hear them puff when they come to the surface.

VISITOR: What we were wondering about is how they manage to sleep. Seems like they'd drown if they just settled down on the bottom for a snooze.

LOCAL: Oh, they're not that dumb. When night comes they just flop up on the beach and sleep 'til dawn.

VISITOR: So that's how they do it. I asked several people out at the beach, but nobody seemed to know. On television they seem real friendly. Don't guess the wild ones are dangerous, are they?

LOCAL: Not as long as they are just swimming around, but if you ever come up on a bunch out on the beach and wake 'em up they can get pretty mean. You know they got a mouthful of big teeth and they can bite your leg off with one snap.

VISITOR: Great guns! I never knew that. Not a very smart idea to go walking along the beach at night, then, is it?

LOCAL: Not much to worry about. They generally pick a spot where people hardly ever go.

VISITOR: Well, you've answered a question I've wondered about ever since I first started seeing that show on television. I've asked a lot of people, but nobody had the answer. Guess you just naturally learn about such things when you live close to the water.

The visitor had found a "knowledgeable" native and I wondered as the two walked back up toward the parking lot what other gems of wisdom were being offered. How, I wondered, could anyone have spent the better part of his life on the coast and still be so abysmally ignorant about a creature that had gained such widespread popularity? If he had simply admitted that he did not know the answer, his lack of knowledge could have been overlooked.

It is a good case in point to prove that some people simply cannot resist giving an answer, no matter how wrong it may be. Of the two, I would rate the visitor as having a superior I.Q. He had, at least, asked an intelligent question. It can only be hoped that before he returned to Kansas or Ohio, or wherever he came from, he decided to verify his newfound "knowledge" from a more reliable source.

Almost without exception, every creature in the sea is in constant peril of falling prey to some other creature that wishes to make a meal of it. Most depend entirely on speed and alertness to escape the jaws of their natural predators; others rely on tricks of camouflage and skilled ability to conceal themselves quickly. Porpoise and their larger relatives, the killer whales, show decided traits that indicate they will band together for mutual protection and work as a team in obtaining food. Below the mammals, however, it is almost certain that no sea creature has even the faintest concern for the safety of its own kind.

Through aeons of adaptation a relatively few forms of sea animals have developed armament that causes their would-be enemies to avoid them. These weapons may be in the form of venomous spines or fangs and, in some cases, stinging tentacles. Occasionally such armament serves a dual purpose—one, to ward off attack and two, to assist in gathering food. There are other animals that are clad in armor strictly for the protection of the creature inside. Here, the common oyster is a good example of an animal that would seem to be completely protected by its shell. It is limited in protection, however, because some larger creatures can crush it. Others, such as the starfish, can pull it open, and, if he escapes these predators, the little oyster drill can bore a hole through the thick shell and devour the entire oyster.

The sea is a watery jungle where the law of "survival of the fittest" is constantly enforced. There is no suggestion of mercy shown to the injured, the dull-witted, or those infirmed by age. In many cases it appears nature has decreed that only by excessive proliferation are certain types permitted to continue.

It is remarkable that the frail human invader of this aquatic jungle is relatively safe from harm. It is not because he is feared by those inhabitants powerful enough to subdue him. From these, his general safety lies in the fact that he is not a natural form of food. Infrequently, large rapacious creatures, notably certain sharks, will elect to sample a human. Whether the attack is made by mistaken identity or curiosity, the results are often tragic.

But, it is not the spectacular attacks by large creatures that account for most of mankind's injuries. Rather, most people are hurt and occasionally killed by the smaller forms of sea life. Usually these encounters are the result of lack of awareness on the part of the human and the inability to recognize potential danger before blundering into it. No one with even a sketchy knowledge of the forest would be foolish enough to try to capture a porcupine with his bare hands or molest a nest of hornets, but for some reason that same person is prone to let down his guard when he enters the sea.

It is probably because, during his occasional and brief ventures into the salt water, he has learned that almost everything that comes within his grasp is practically harmless. He has found that in most cases he can casually pick up any seashell that attracts his attention, just as he can catch a living seahorse or starfish and take it back to the dry sand to examine it more closely. Also soon discovered is the fact that most jellyfish, chunks of coral, and sponges may be handled without harmful effects. Man found that even some fish are so slow-moving that they are easy to grab and hold with the bare hand. Good examples are some of the swellfish, especially if one learns that the prickly feeling represents no injury. When removed with a light touch they are an object of interest as they inflate their bodies with air. And, there are numerous others that may be taken alive, dried, and kept as curios.

It has often been noted that when a person learns to fly a plane he goes through distinct phases. When he makes his first solo flight he is decidedly cautious for the following few flights. The next stage is reached when he has developed enough skill to feel confident and this is the danger period, because he is apt to attempt maneuvers beyond his ability. If he survives a couple of narrow escapes, the chances are he will steady down and become a competent pilot. There is a close analogy where flying and exploring the salt water are concerned.

With so many comparatively innocuous living specimens to handle without fear, man becomes increasingly bold and the temptation to touch, and occasionally grasp, other creatures continues to grow. It should always be remembered, however, that scattered about in the throngs of harmless life, there are certain to be a few that are dangerous. It is wise to avoid contact with any sea creature until its potential is known.

There are certain to be those who will maintain they have been fishing and swimming for years and the only time they have been injured was by accidentally stepping on the ragged edge of a broken bottle. They will find no argument here, because this is the rule, rather than the exception. Such a boast, however, is more a matter of luck for some, while with others it may be the result of either deliberately or subconsciously following common sense rules of caution. Then, too, it cannot be denied that many people will escape injury by only the narrowest margin and never have any idea just how close they came to serious injury. If all of the creatures mentioned in this book were gathered along a given stretch of the coast it would be a decidedly dangerous region.

Fortunately, such a condition could hardly exist, because those that may be numerous in one area are seldom found in others. Still further, some may be relatively close by, but not in waters frequented by the average human. There is always the possibility, however, that for some unexplained reason, certain sea creatures will show up where they are least expected.

Because of the vastness of the sea it is a treacherous practice to try to establish hard and fast rules about any of its inhabitants. Even in this so-called enlightened age, it has been reliably estimated that only about half of the forms of sea life have been cataloged. And this estimate is not restricted to tiny and supposedly insignificant creatures. Even large fish that science has been convinced are either extinct or confined to abyssal depths are occasionally found to still be in existence, or present in waters where they have heretofore been unexpected.

Perhaps the most outstanding example of this was the startling discovery of the coelacanth. Paleozoologists were certain this large fish vanished some fifty million years ago. Yet, in 1938, Miss M. Courtenay-Latimer, curator of a museum in East London, Union of South Africa, was called to the waterfront to identify an unknown specimen of a fish which local fishermen had reported catching. Upon viewing the creature, Miss Latimer immediately suspected it was something highly unusual. She wasted little time in passing on the details to the renowned ichthyologist Dr. J. L. B. Smith. When still another coelacanth was caught and preserved by refrigeration, Dr. Smith had an opportunity to examine it in minute detail and to compare it with fossils of this ancient fish. He proved beyond a shadow of a doubt that this fish, supposedly extinct for so many millions of years, was still alive. It had simply escaped the notice of scientists. Subsequent catches of other coelacanths convinced the skeptics and an entire chapter in marine biology had to be rewritten. Its discovery served to amplify the reluctance of the sea to disclose its secrets.

Still another somewhat similar discovery was made in 1947 when Thor Heyerdahl and his five companions crossed 4,300 miles of the Pacific Ocean on the raft *Kon Tiki*. Not one, but two snake mackerel jumped aboard the craft on separate occasions. It was the first time anyone had reported seeing this fish alive. They were known to exist, but it was believed they lived only at great depths. Skeletal remains were all that had ever been found, yet those that boarded the raft suggested that they are also found near the surface, at least during the dark hours of night.

Accounts of other fish, either supposed to have vanished ages ago, or to be restricted to one specific geographic region, confounded science by revealing themselves where least expected. The truth is, when one stops to reflect on the fact that man has yet to fully chart the land on which he lives, there is little wonder that contradictions about the countless forms of sea life will continue to occur. It is risky to make positive statements about the range of any sea creature.

A decidedly safer course, when speaking of first one type and then another, is to say they are *known* to be indigenous to a given region, but still leave the door ajar for subsequent investigation. Research may have proven that a specific species is numerous in a given area, but it does not necessarily follow that this same creature is absolutely confined to that locale. Rather, it may simply mean that a complete investigation has not been conducted at other places.

A popular misconception concerning the numerous branches of science is that once a fact has been recorded, it becomes irrevocably true. In general, the modern scientist waits until enough verifiable evidence is presented to permit a logical conclusion to be drawn. Quite unlike his predecessors of a century ago, he is well aware that tomorrow, or a year from now, new discoveries will be made.

Another erroneous but widely accepted belief is that scientists are a class of people unto themselves. They are frequently pictured as stuffy old men, smugly convinced they know all that is to be known. Regrettably, there are still a few of these old guard academicians who seemingly dwell in an ivory tower, intoning dogmas in esoteric terms understood only by those who specialize in their branch of science. Admittedly, this waning minority is still reluctant to accept the word of anyone save those formally educated in their selected field.

It may be stated without fear of contradiction that such pedantic individuals are indeed rare in the science of marine biology. The truly dedicated student knows that he alone, or several thousand of his colleagues, could not possibly discover and thoroughly study all there is to know. As a rule, these scientists are not only receptive but they genuinely welcome the layman who intelligently offers interesting information. It may be in the form of an unusual specimen or the description of some sea creature far removed from its supposedly natural range. Again, it may be a recognizable species that has been observed to behave in a decidedly atypical manner.

Occasionally the angler, skin diver, or someone exploring a section of coastal waters will manage to capture and adequately preserve a creature he has every right to believe is unusual in some respect. His natural impulse is to hurry to the nearest marine laboratory and display his find. In most cases it can be quickly identified, but there is always the chance that he has actually dredged up something unusual. There are no monetary rewards if such should be the case, but there is a distinct sense of personal satisfaction that comes with such a discovery.

In all fairness, however, it should be remembered that any marine laboratory is almost certainly understaffed. Those who work there generally have weeks and months of important work already waiting to be done. While it is one of the services of such laboratories to function as information centers, this does not mean that the resident scientists are eagerly awaiting any and every occasional visitor who has found a fish, worm, or shell that has him puzzled.

A more practical approach is to first engage in a reasonable amount of on-the-scene investigation. Commercial fishermen who have spent years at their trade in a given region are frequently surprisingly dependable sources of general marine information. They are seldom knowledgeable of scientific names, or capable of expounding on class, order, family, and genus, but they can generally look at a creature and tell whether or not it is common to the environs of their bailiwick and they will usually be able to supply the local name.

Of course, there is always the possibility of first making contact with someone gifted with the "expertise" of the aforementioned porpoise expert. It is therefore a wise practice to ask several people in the locality—not all in one group at a single fish house. If it is the general consensus that your find is unusual, it is then reasonable to assume the nearest marine laboratory will be interested.

Under normal conditions it is almost impossible to keep the specimen alive. If it is to be given serious attention it should be preserved in as nearly a natural state as possible. This is most easily and practically accomplished—on a short-term basis—by keeping the specimen packed in ice.

One final word of caution that should always be observed pertains to the careless handling of any creature not known to be harmless. The layman-investigator should studiously avoid the temptation to toss caution aside and grab his find with bare hands. A far safer practice is to scoop it up with a net. A pair of metal tongs or long-nosed fish grippers are valuable if the specimen must be handled.

It is almost certain that some who read this will interpret it as an attempt to write a scare book, contrived to leave the reader with the impression that every time he puts his foot in the water there is some evil creature just waiting to do him harm. On the contrary, the primary aim is to simply point out potential hazards that exist today just as they did before the dawn of history.

Most can be avoided if suggested precautionary measures are observed, but it is also important to know what to expect when injury does occur. Whenever practical, the generally recognized forms of first-aid treatment are described. If a person is to be realistic, he must acknowledge the sea as an alien world and mankind as an uninvited interloper.

2

Drifting, Creeping, and Waiting

Portuguese Man-of-War

The Portuguese man-of-war, *Physalia physalis,* is a sea creature that is as interesting as it is dangerous. They are frequently found drifting on the surface in large numbers, with "fleets" of fifty to well over a hundred not being unusual. When viewed from the surface they resemble an assortment of translucent balloons. These floats are known as pneumatophores and are bluish in color, ranging in size from a man's clinched fist to almost as large as a football. On the dorsal side it appears that a crest has been sewn on from bow to stern to serve as a sail. This crest, like the balloon, is almost clear with a thin pink border along the upper edge.

In many respects these creatures are similar to jellyfish, but are sufficiently different to be classified in a separate order known as Siphonophora. Only the balloon portion of this oddity is visible from the surface and, like an iceberg, it is the part below that is the most dangerous.

The Portuguese man-of-war are members of the phylum Coelenterata and are closely related to jellyfish, sea anemones, and coral. Thus, like coral and other members of this group, they are not a single animal, but a collection of countless small creatures banded together to form what appears to be an individual unit.

Portuguese man-of-war.

Trailing beneath the gas-filled balloon are scores of pale bluish tentacles that sometimes reach a length of seventy-five feet or more. It is these wispy, threadlike tentacles that collect food for the colony of tiny animals that cluster about the base of the floats. The tentacles are muscular and contract when food is captured, drawing it upward so that it may be fed upon by the complex organ that constitutes the mouth of the colony.

Each of the tentacles is equipped with numerous nematocysts, or microscopic stinging cells, scattered along the length. These tiny cells are motivated into instant reflex action when touched by a fish or other living creature. If the contact happens to be a human's arm, leg, or the entire body, the action is the same. It is not that the man-of-war would attempt to feed on a human, or any other large creature, because the normal diet consists of small fish and other, often minute, forms of sea life. The tentacles will begin to contract only if the victim is light enough to be supported by the float.

It is because the nematocysts attached to the tentacles are activated instinctively when touched that they represent a danger to humans. Only when the individual nematocyst is magnified and examined under laboratory conditions is one able to fully comprehend the complex design and understand why the man-of-war is so dangerous to humans.

Each of the stinging cells may be compared to a tiny, almost hollow, bead. Contained inside these nematocysts is a wisp of a thread that is tipped with a barb, needle-sharp and shaped like the tip of a harpoon. The thread is coiled and tense, much like a confined spring. Each remains "cocked" until stimulated by contact with some object. At that instant the reaction is immediate. The tension is released, allowing the venom-conducting spring to dart out of an almost infinitesimal orifice in the same manner as a harpoon being shot from a gun.

As many as several hundred of these poisonous darts may enter the flesh in a matter of seconds. So fragile are the lines to which the darts are attached, that even a small minnow could easily break free were it not for a powerful and fast-acting venom that is neurotoxic in property, similar to the venom of a cobra and other snakes whose poison attacks the nerve centers. The effect is almost instant paralyzation that renders a small creature helpless before escape is possible.

The man-of-war does not depend on a single tentacle for the complete capture. Instead, when first stung, the victim's movement causes it to encounter several other tentacles and still more darts are released. These food-gathering strands are so numerous as to resemble hairs from a human head. Thus, while some forms of sea life are just being collected, others are being drawn upward, while up at the top the colonial mouth is digesting still another victim.

There have been reports that human swimmers have died as a result of extensive contact with the man-of-war—probably when trying to swim through a group of them. It may be that a human even in the best of health could be sufficiently envenomated as to die and it may be that the reported victims had some physical condition that was aggravated by the poison.

Even to have part of the body stung can, and often does, produce serious results. At times, depending upon the extent of contact, hospitalization is necessary. Again, the human victim may suffer pain, but be able to throw off the effects without medical aid.

There are few, if any, substitutes for personal exposure to an experience. I have been acquainted with the man-of-war since early childhood. From time to time I have been mildly stung when handling fishing lines that have been drawn through a mass of tentacles. Not only had I been warned but I had often warned newcomers to the beach to beware of these creatures. Some years ago, however, I began to wonder if the extent of direct contact was as painful as everyone said. To settle the question I decided to make a personal test.

It was an impulsive prank that I was to regret with the suddenness that comes to someone who puts his finger in an electric socket—just to see what it feels like. I was swimming alone in the Gulf of Mexico when I spotted a fleet of man-of-war some distance from shore. One had drifted off from the main group and I recall thinking this would be a good chance to make my Dr. Jekyll experiment.

My intention had been to brush the tentacles with my hand and part of my forearm, but I must have misjudged due to some error in depth perception or the unexpected thrust of a wave. Whatever, I encountered a much larger mass than I had intended. Instead of a controlled experiment, I suddenly realized I had covered my entire arm and part of my shoulder with the streaming tentacles.

The awareness of pain was as sudden as it was intense. Years earlier I had tried the finger-in-the-electric-socket, but at the time it was on a dry wooden floor and the tingle was fleeting. In some respects my contact with the Portuguese man-of-war was comparable to an electric jolt, except that it grew more intense as I hastily withdrew. Sensing that I had acted unwisely, I began swimming rapidly toward the beach. Although I was in excellent physical condition and a better than average swimmer, I discovered I was rapidly losing muscular control and I began to wonder if I was going to maintain sufficient coordination long enough to keep from drowning.

When I did reach shallow water I staggered and fell several times before I was safely out on the beach. Although I was no longer in danger of drowning, I found myself becoming dizzy and engulfed in severe pains that seemed centered in my armpits and groin. Breathing was swiftly becoming increasingly labored, as if a band was being drawn tighter and tighter around my chest. My fingers and toes were tingling and when I tried to flex them it seemed as if they were paralyzed.

I was on a deserted stretch of beach, but if someone had been only a hundred yards away I could not have called for help, because even gasping, shallow breaths were almost more than I could manage.

The severity of the pain and related problems persisted for well over an hour. Then gradually, as the effects of Novocain from a dental hypodermic diminish, so did the results of my Jekyllian experiment. I found I was able to get to my feet and walk in an erratic fashion. By the time I reached a marina I had regained reasonable control of my body. My arm, hand, and shoulder still pained as if only that section of my body had been subjected to a bad sunburn.

Ahead was a sleek cabin boat owned by an old charter captain with whom I had often fished. Climbing aboard I sat on the edge of the fishbox and related the account of my folly. The skipper was obviously disgusted and subjected me to a verbal chastisement, as he swabbed the area of pain with alcohol. The treatment afforded some relief, but it was not until the following afternoon that the stinging sensation completely subsided.

Despite my fairly rapid recovery, subsequent investigation has disclosed that coastal hospitals are occasionally called upon to treat victims more extensively. Oxygen therapy is frequently employed to alleviate respiratory constriction. Analgesics and calcium gluconate have been found effective and calamine lotion is used to reduce surface pain.

In first-aid treatment, the primary step is to remove any of the pieces of tentacles that still adhere to the skin. In doing so, caution should be used to avoid further injury to the affected area, as well as parts of the skin that have not already been stung. Even someone assisting in this phase of first aid may be injured, because any of the nematocysts which have not already discharged their venom remain "cocked" for a considerable length of time.

If the victim is in good physical condition and has brushed against only a few of the tentacles, the results may be only an unpleasant stinging sensation, with the discomfort passing away in an hour or two. More extensive contact, coupled with various health problems, can have more serious effects.

Danger from the Portuguese man-of-war is not restricted entirely to contact in the water. Occasionally a fleet of them will be close to the shallow water. If they are in this position and a sudden squall, with onshore winds, develops, the resulting high waves may drive large numbers of them well beyond the tide line. The floats are quite often carried up to the jumble of wrack far back up on the beach.

After the storm has passed the smooth surface near the water may appear as an inviting place for sunbathers to recline. What cannot be seen is the veritable cobweb mesh consisting of broken tentacles. It is of no consequence that they have been torn away from the floats. The individual microscopic nematocysts remain potent for hours until the hot rays of the sun cause them to dry up and decay. If it were possible to select a small area and subject it to sufficient magnification, the stinging cells would be seen lying in a helter-skelter fashion.

Many of the tiny beads would have stopped with the openings pointing down toward the sand, some would be lying on their sides, while others would be pointing upward. While still damp and alive, just a light touch will trigger the reflex action of the venomous darts. Considering that they may be present in astronomical numbers, it should be obvious that a good percentage of them will enter any bare flesh that contacts them.

In most cases the extent of envenomation is considerably less than if contact were made in open water, but sunbathers occasionally find themselves becoming uncomfortable from a puzzling yet painful rash. If numerous still-inflated balloons are to be seen in the wrack line, those wishing to stretch out on the sand would do well to spread a blanket before doing so.

The pneumatophores, or floats, are frequently a source of curiosity to those not accustomed to seeing them. There is a temptation to pick them up for closer scrutiny, but they would do well to exercise caution. The balloons are inflated with a toxic gas that can cause injury to the eyes if ruptured so that a blast is directed toward the face.

Since small fish constitute a part of the man-of-war's diet, it seems improbable that any fish would deliberately make its home in and around the cluster of trailing tentacles. As is so frequently the case in almost all forms of nature, there is an exception to the rule. Such an exception here is the fish commonly known as the bluebottle fish, *Nomeus gronovii*. It is a little jacklike fish with a silver body, marked with vertical blue stripes.

Why it seems to deliberately choose such a dangerous habitat is not fully understood. It was long believed the fish was immune to the venom of the nematocysts, acting as a Lorelei to lure other fish into the death trap. More extensive investigation has proved, however, that while these little fish may possess some degree of immunity to the venomous darts, they can be killed by the poison.

The bluebottle fish appears content to depend upon its agility in avoiding the tentacles. It is perhaps urged to continue its hazardous abode, rewarded only by protection from larger fish.

Scuba diving affords an excellent opportunity to observe these little fish as they dart about in the streaming tentacles, seemingly with careless abandon. At times they will stray off to the side for several feet, only to beat a hasty retreat if a larger fish approaches. At times other small fry will follow the bluebottle, only to be instantly stunned and drawn slowly upward toward the mouth. It has been suggested that these little fish may be willing to court such danger in exchange for food that has been dropped from the man-of-war. There may be some truth in this, but I have never observed it. And, since the man-of-war feeds by absorbing the flesh of its victims, there would be little wasted, save for tiny bones and scales.

While it is only my own personal theory, I am inclined to believe that the bluebottle fish finds its own food in adjacent waters. I believe it uses the dangerous tentacles much as a rabbit will seek the safety of a briarpatch when danger threatens.

Oddly enough, the Portuguese man-of-war is not without some ability to choose its own course. Entire fleets of these creatures have been observed to adjust their position in the water so that their sail is set at such an angle as to cause them to change direction, much as a sailboat will come about to sail on another tack. To someone casually observing such a mass maneuver, it can almost be believed that the "flagship" has issued orders for a change of course. It is beyond the bounds of rational thinking to even suppose that such lowly creatures would be capable of communication. A more logical answer is that the sensory organs are all attuned to changes in water temperature and depth. Instinct must therefore dictate that a change of direction is in order if they are to avoid the disaster of being washed ashore or grounded on a shallow water reef.

Still another oddity concerning the self-preservation of these siphonophora may be observed when a group is floating on the surface of almost motionless water. Prolonged exposure to the sun causes the gas-filled pneumatophores to dry. Under normal conditions there is enough chop to the waves to keep them thoroughly damp and elastic. However, when subjected to an extended period of flat calm, these paper-thin floats would be increasingly vulnerable to developing a leak. Of course, if this should happen the entire colony would perish with the sinking that would follow.

To prevent such a disaster the unit begins shifting its ballast to an extent that the balloon rolls over so far that even the sail is lying flat on the water. When one side is sufficiently damp, the procedure is reversed and the float is soaked on the opposite side. Then, when some form of instinct reassures the colony that their ship is seaworthy again, it returns to a normal position and continues on its course.

Such seemingly intelligent behavior would appear as involuntary as the opening and closing of certain flowers at specified times during a twenty-four-hour period. However, such plants are governed by sunlight or, in some cases, the absence of it, but *Physalia* acts in such a manner only when the need becomes apparent. It remains one of the riddles of nature how a colony consisting of creatures of such low order are able to foresee danger. Still more, how they are able to work as a team in executing measures to prevent it. Such action serves to reinforce the fact that as the human store of knowledge increases about a given subject, additional questions arise to further perplex the investigator.

Jellyfish

Anyone in any part of the world who swims in the surf, strolls along the beach, skin-dives, or goes fishing in bays or oceans is almost certain to have observed jellyfish. They know, or have heard from reliable sources, that some kinds are dangerous because of their ability to sting. The name "jellyfish" is misleading since they are not fish any more than is a chunk of coral. They are more properly known as jellies, such as the blueplate jelly, moon jelly, and many, many more. However, the misnomer is ingrained in the language and will probably remain so. It will occasionally be used herein when used in general terms.

Considering the vast numbers of different types of jellies it is indeed fortunate that most are not capable of inflicting injury to humans. Yet, there are some that produce a mild stinging rash on human skin. Still fewer are rated as capable of delivering painful injury, while a very few are considered to be exceedingly dangerous. At least one type has been called the most dangerous creature in the sea. This latter is known by several common names that include the fire medusa, box jelly, and sea wasp. Scientifically, they are known as *Chironex fleckeri*, and it is reported that people have died in a matter of minutes after contact with them.

Jellies with long-trailing tentacles are more properly called medusas. The name comes from the Greek legend of the once beautiful maiden, famed for her long tresses, who eventually became a frightful sea monster. Unlike the mythological Medusa who turned people into stone, the jelly medusas have made many humans feel that a portion of their body has been seared with a blowtorch.

All jellyfish, like the Portuguese man-of-war, are members of the phylum Coelenterata and are among the most primitive organisms. Although many are firm enough to be handled freely, all are over 98 percent water and are similar to globs of congealed gelatin.

While they are complex in some minor aspects, the average jellyfish is little more than a stomach surrounded by a mouth. In general, they are creatures of the open sea and may be found either on the surface or below for thousands of feet. Many common forms are round in shape with the top resembling an umbrella or shallow bowl. The concave underside is hollow and their method of movement is accomplished by rhythmical pulsing movement of the entire body.

As the bowl relaxes, water fills the hollow underside, muscles around the rim contract, and as the water is forced out, the jelly moves. This feeble method of locomotion enables them to inch their way along through the water. If caught in strong tides or driven shoreward by wave action they are automatically in trouble. If they happen to be of a stinging type, human swimmers may also be in trouble, because they will

Moon jelly (bottom), blueplate jelly.

be carried into the marginal waters where people are likely
to be swimming.

At times, prolonged onshore winds, with the resulting high
waves, will leave a section of the beach strewn with varying
numbers of them. When such conditions exist it is well to
resist the temptation to pick them up until it has been established they are of an innocuous species. Like the Portuguese
man-of-war, some are capable of producing stings even after
being stranded.

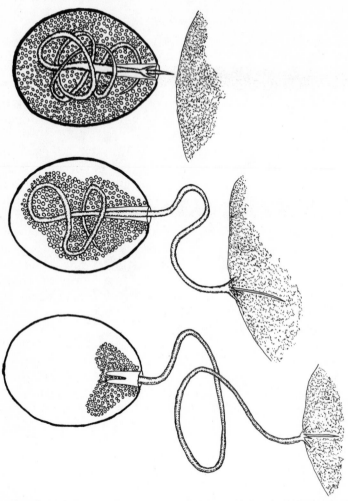

Details of microscopic nematocyst. (Top) Cocked nematocyst, (middle) partly dislodged, (bottom) harpoon line fully expelled and venom injected.

In order to collect food, many forms of jellies depend upon threadlike tentacles that hang down from the underside. Again, like *Physalia*, the tentacles are armed with batteries of nematocysts that are used to stun plankton, larval fishes, crabs, and other small forms of sea life.

One of the most familiar jellies found in Atlantic waters is the purple or moon jelly, *Aurelia aurita.* It is a circular disk and the average size is about a foot in diameter. Viewed from above, it displays a cluster of four rings at the center of the blue-tinted body and there is a fringe of short tentacles around the perimeter. These tentacles are equipped with conventional stinging cells, but the venom is not of sufficient potency to be painful to humans.

Decidedly more objectionable is the big blueplate jelly, *Cyanea capillata,* which reaches about a foot and a half in width. The rim is not as circular as *Aurelia,* having a somewhat scalloped edge and the tentacles are much longer. The stinging cells, or nematocysts, contain a poison that can inflict burning pain to human flesh. Fortunately, polar waters are not popular for human swimmers, because closely related to the blueplates in those frigid waters is *Cyanea arcticia,* occasionally reaching a diameter of nine feet with tentacles well over a hundred feet long. At least one of these giant jellies, measuring seven and a half feet across, was collected in the waters off Massachusetts.

If a person contacts any kind of jellyfish and develops a stinging rash, he is naturally prone to wonder if the species is actually dangerous or simply annoying. At this point it is well to mention that some people are more sensitive to certain types of venom, while many others feel little or no unpleasant effects.

The term "sea nettle" is perhaps the one most widely used for jellies found around the world in all tropical and temperate salt waters. It is found from the southern tip of Africa and north as far as New York. The sea nettle, *Dactylometra quinquecirrha,* measures about eight inches across, is somewhat milky in basic color with decided pink marks and bright yellow tentacles. A close relative in the Pacific, both north and south of the equator, is *Dactylometra pacificus.* The same size applies to the nettle of both oceans, but the color is quite different. The Pacific species has a purple ground color with black markings and black tentacles. Both species are capable of producing intense pain.

Atlantic (left) and Pacific sea nettles.

Logically, the degree of pain from any stinging jellyfish depends to a large extent on the number of nematocysts that have discharged their poison into the flesh. The extent of the injury is frequently amplified by the natural impulse to get out of the water and wipe away the offending threads as quickly as possible. It is important to bear in mind that following this course of action is precisely what should *not* be done. The cobweb of tentacles is certain to contain countless nematocysts that have not yet released their stinging darts. Rubbing the flesh causes the victim to continue the process of envenomation.

There are two methods that can drastically restrict the extent of additional injury. It can only be hoped that one or the other of the first-aid necessities is close at hand. Any type of alcohol is best because it instantly stuns any stinging cell it touches. Second best is almost any drying agent that can be dusted on the body. Talcum powder is good, but if this is not available there are several substitutes. These may be in the form of ashes from a dead beach fire, dust scooped up from the edge of a road, or even fine dry sand. Any type of powder should be sprinkled on the skin, but not rubbed. After all moisture is gone the threads can be carefully picked off.

One of the problems often encountered with stinging jellyfish is that the person may swim into an area where they are numerous. He is lucky if he can retreat in the right direction instead of blundering into an even denser concentration of tentacles.

When the degree of contact is moderate the first awareness will be a stinging or burning sensation, much as if part of the body were showered with tiny sparks. Occasionally, the flesh will develop a burning rash and the victim may complain of muscular pain, especially noticeable in the groin and armpits. Vomiting and excessive perspiration are not uncommon symptoms.

When anyone has been even moderately stung by jellyfish he should stay out of the water for a while, even though the initial pain has subsided. Continuing to swim should be avoided because of the possible danger of a secondary shock. This may come in the form of severe cramps or mild toxicosis. Ashore, such reaction may simply be annoying, but if swimming, the victim may lose control and drown. A waiting period of at least an hour is wise. During that time it can be determined whether or not any aftereffects may be forthcoming.

Obviously, avoiding contact with stinging jellyfish is the most logical way to prevent an unpleasant experience. If any of the noxious species are present it is quite likely that many more will be nearby. The infestation will likely be of short duration and it is just common sense to stay ashore until the water is clear.

Sea wasp.

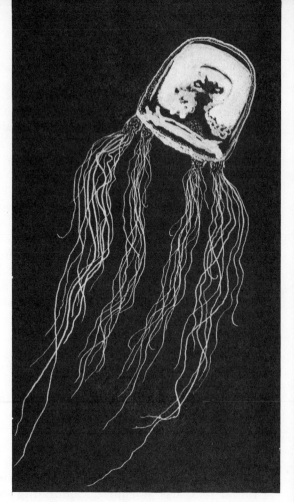

The sea wasp, box jelly, or fire medusas are simply different names for the same creature. As previously mentioned,
they have been called the most dangerous creatures mankind
is likely to encounter in the sea. Admittedly, this is debatable
when certain sharks and other animals are considered. However, the violent sting of the sea wasp, *Chironex fleckeri*, has
been known to cause death in a matter of minutes. Their
range is restricted primarily to waters along the north coast of
Australia.

Another close relative, *Chiropsalmus quadrigatus*, is found
northward as far as the Philippines. Like *C. fleckeri*, they are

known as cubomedusae, so called because of their somewhat cube shape. Experiments on mice under laboratory conditions have established that the venom of the sea wasp is several hundred times more virulent than that of the Portuguese man-of-war.

They are about as large as an average-sized grapefruit and pale blue in color. Unlike most jellyfish, the sea wasp is a fast swimmer, able to propel itself through the water in a darting fashion. Fortunately, they are not numerous, but contact with only one can cause swift death. Even a mild brush can cause intense pain and the only recourse is to get the victim to a hospital in the shortest possible time.

As with other jellyfish, the sea wasp is found in inshore waters only occasionally. At times they will invade the shallow water along a particular beach, yet be completely absent for many miles in either direction. Because of their ability to move rapidly, they are not nearly so subject to becoming captives of currents and waves. It can only be assumed they venture shoreward of their own volition; probably in pursuit of a certain type of food.

A distant relative of the sea wasp is occasionally found in the western Atlantic and various other parts of the world. They bear a distinct resemblance to those of the western Pacific, but their danger is not nearly so great.

Anemones

Sea anemones are coelenterates of the order Madreporaria and are found in many parts of the sea. A few are capable of inflicting painful stings. Many varieties are quite colorful and bear a resemblance to a flower growing on the top of a thick stalk. The anemone's stinging cells are contained in tentacles which wave about, waiting for some small creature to swim into them.

One of the most colorful sea anemones, *Sagartia elegans,* is occasionally found near the base of sponges. When a diver cuts the sponge loose his hand will likely come in contact with the tentacles of the anemone. Because of hypersensitiv-

Sea anemone.

ity or repeated contact, the diver may develop a swollen hand, headache, and vomiting. Often the victim is said to have "sponge fisherman's disease," when, in reality, the sponge has nothing to do with it.

Other species of anemones with a yen for travel will often affix themselves to the carapace of crabs. In exchange for the free transportation afforded by their host, the anemone provides the crab with added protection. Species of anemones are numerous with some inhabiting shallow water, while others may be found at a depth of several miles.

Coral

Coral is found in many forms and is one of the most important of the colonial animals, since various types are responsible for building reefs and atolls. In many cases the continued growth forms the base of islands.

Old coral, which forms the foundation for the new growth, is harmful only to ships that may run aground on it; often with disastrous results. The new growth of this rocklike substance is often sharp enough to produce serious cuts and gashes to the flesh of human swimmers. The coral polyps extract lime from sea water and thus form a rigid "skeleton."

The needle-sharp points of some varieties of coral contain stinging cells that not only lacerate flesh but produce wounds that are slow to heal.

Resembling branches or the antlers of an elk is the so-called elkhorn coral. It is actually a hydrocoral of the order Milleporina. Close examination will show a profusion of fine hairs that coat the branches. To touch any part of this hydrocoral is to drive countless stinging spines into the flesh.

Coral reef.

The effect is an intense burning sensation. The nettles are not dangerous, but one encounter is sufficient to cause the swimmer or skin diver to leave it alone in the future. The intense burning sensation is usually of short duration and the pain diminishes rapidly.

Cuts and scrapes from any coral may cause secondary infection. Because of this, the wound should be washed promptly and the use of any mild antiseptic is recommended.

Sponges

Sponges are of the phylum Porifera. Many species are of commercial value and are harmless. There are at least two types, however, that should be avoided. One of these is the fire sponge and the other is the bun sponge.

The fire sponge, *Tadania ignis,* is also known as the red sponge. It is widespread in tropical waters and not uncommon off the lower coast of Florida. (The Latin name *ignis* means fire.) It is irregular in shape with numerous fingerlike branches. It is of no commercial value, but the shape and color cause it to be attractive to unwary collectors.

Those who yield to the temptation to take the entire sponge, or break off part of it, do not have long to wait before experiencing the first symptoms. They begin with a painful itching similar to contact with poison ivy. Several hours may pass before the fingers and occasionally the entire hand begin to swell and become nearly immovable. Attempts to flex the fingers produce added pain.

The effects, especially that of aching, may remain for as long as one or two days, after which the edema subsides and moving the fingers is no longer painful. Diluted acetic acid has frequently been found beneficial in reducing the effects of the poison.

The bun sponge, *Fibulia nolitangere,* should also be left alone. Here again, the Latin word *nolitangere* is appropriate; loosely translated it means "do not touch." The bun is usually restricted to waters deep enough not to involve swimmers and the drab brown color does not invite the attention of collectors. As its common name implies, it is rounded like a bun. It generally causes trouble only for skin divers who accidentally bump into it while exploring the bottom. The symptoms and treatment are the same as for the fire sponge.

Sea Urchins

Sea urchins are echinoderms and are closely related to starfish, sea cucumbers, and sea lilies. Certain ones of these creatures bear a striking resemblance to plant life, but they are marine animals with limy plates that serve as skeletons. Of the echinoderms, only certain sea urchins and several species of Pacific starfish may be considered dangerous.

A few species of sea urchins can inflict painful puncture wounds, while even fewer are poisonous. The dangerous ones are found in tropical waters and the venomous spines contain poison fluid that ranges from painfully irritating to some species that have been reported to cause death when extensive contact has been made.

Only occasionally will the surf bather encounter a poisonous sea urchin. Skin divers are more likely prospects to be hurt, and there are times when the damage is done before the victim realizes he is in the presence of danger.

Like starfish, sea urchins move about the bottom—some almost constantly. At a snail's pace, they inch their way along in quest of food. Wading fishermen, especially those who stalk the shallow flats in search of inshore game fish, should exercise caution. The spines of some urchins are so sharp they will easily penetrate the canvas sides of gym shoes and cause painful injury when they puncture the flesh.

The name echinoderm comes from the Greek *echinus* and refers to their armor of spines. It was used interchangeably for both sea urchins and hedgehogs, the latter being similar to the New World porcupine. Running afoul of a dangerous sea urchin can produce painful results, not unlike an encounter with a porcupine. Most porcupines will either make an effort to get out of your path or make their presence

Common sea urchin.

known by the rustle of quills. Their underwater counterpart is not so obliging. It just sits there and if you run into it, you pay the penalty.

The closest view of a sea urchin many visitors to beach areas ever have is the globelike skeleton in a curio shop or washed up on the shore. Examination will show this to resemble a thin-shelled ball that resembles a tomato in shape. On the underside is a hole that once housed the urchin's teeth which are used to cut various forms of sea grasses. Closer scrutiny of this globe will reveal an interesting and thought-provoking sight. A pattern of five rays that originate on the underside and curve around to the top will be seen.

This suggests that aeons ago the sea urchin was a starfish and somewhere in the evolutionary scheme this group of starfish found reason to curl the legs upward so that the tips pointed toward one another. From here two changes began to develop. The legs, or crawlers, on the underside of the star-fish began to grow longer and calcification filled in the vacant spaces between the upcurved legs so that the skeleton became the globe-shaped structure it is today.

Also noticeable on the ball are scores of tiny pockmarks that show where the spines were attached to the body. In a living specimen, the sea urchin may be likened to a pin cushion, except that the pins are reversed so that the sharp ends point outward. The spines differ from one species to another. Most are short with dull or rounded tips. They are prickly to the touch, and some may even be stepped on with a bare foot without serious injury.

Still another variety, generally known as long-spined urchins, have longer and more pointed spines. While not poisonous, they are sharp and stiff enough to easily penetrate the flesh. Because they are brittle, they often break off, leaving part of the spine imbedded. Those that do not break off beneath the skin can be pulled out and the only danger is the same as any other puncture wound.

When the spine breaks beneath the skin and is so deeply imbedded that it cannot be extracted with a pair of tweezers, it becomes necessary to visit a physician. He will have to probe for the broken portion and remove it just as would have to be done in extracting a cactus thorn or a splinter. Because they do not contain poison, pain is confined to the point of entry.

One of the most dangerous species is the black sea urchin, *Diadema setosum.* In tropical waters it is almost worldwide, ranging from the east coast of Africa, eastward throughout much of the South Pacific, and north along the coasts of China and Japan. Closely related, if not actually the same, is an almost identical species found around Hawaii, across the eastern Pacific, in the Caribbean and as far north as the southern tip of Florida.

In the adolescent stage the spines are colored with alternating bands of white and dark colors. When fully grown they have turned almost entirely black and the venomous spines may reach nearly a foot in length. They are hollow with exceedingly sharp points. As with all other species, the spines

Black sea urchin.

are simply weapons of defense to protect the urchin from other creatures.

Although they are occasionally a menace to people wading the shallows, they are decidedly more of a threat to skin divers. To bump against one with any part of the body is almost certain to cause painful injury. Not only are the spines filled with venom but, like others of their kind, the spines are brittle and easily broken. Logically, the force with which contact is made dictates the depth of penetration and degree of envenomation.

As is so often the case in encounters with dangerous sea creatures, injury does not always result from lack of knowledge but, rather, the failure to see the noxious creature. Urchins move about in grassy stretches where they may be nearly camouflaged in the waving fronds. Often they will be feeding on lichen that grow on rocks and may be on any part, including the bottom of overhanging ledges.

In their slow roaming they will cross barren areas where the bottom consists of marl or hard-packed sand. In these areas, however, they are easy to spot. At times there will be large groups in a given area and again there may be only a few, or none at all. Fortunately, the least-favored areas are those found most attractive to swimmers. The clear sandy bottom offers little or no food and they avoid places where they are likely to be tossed about by waves.

An interesting sight may at times be noticed when a group of sea urchins, especially those with long sharp quills, are migrating across an open sandy area between their underwater pastures. At such times numerous small fish, frequently of different species, will be traveling with them. The little fish can be seen darting about close to their heavily armored traveling companions. It can only be assumed that the fish are aware of their safety as long as they stay close to the sharp spines. Any larger fish that might attempt to rush in and capture them would run the risk of being impaled.

Certain species of urchins occasionally experience what amounts to a population explosion. Such events occur at irregular intervals and the results are inconsequential, except in an indirect way. Because the urchins feed greedily on bottom grass, they have been known to completely denude large areas during one of these periods of excessive proliferation. Often these grassy stretches are the nursery grounds for numerous valuable food and game fish. When the grass is cut away the protective covering is gone and with it goes the food supply.

Larger fish move in and quickly wipe out the young fish and shrimp. Then, with nothing left to attract them, the larger fish move on to more productive feeding grounds. In a sort of chain reaction, what was a year earlier a favored fishing area quickly becomes a barren stretch of bottom.

Numerous and varied attempts have been made to control

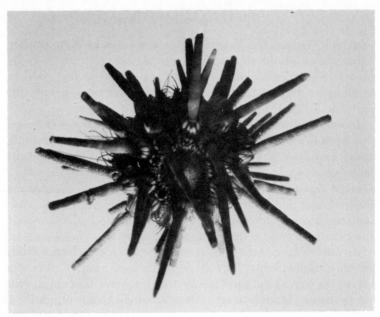

Slate pencil sea urchin.

such rapid reproduction of the sea urchins. Broadcasting of effective chemicals can destroy the urchins but, as is so often the case, man's cure is more serious than the illness. Fortunately, with the growing interest in ecology, man is learning that when he attempts to disturb nature the results frequently have more far-reaching effects than he first suspected.

A still more complex form of stinging apparatus is employed by several other forms of sea urchins. One example, *Toxopneustes pileolus,* is found in Indo-Pacific waters. This urchin is not as large as the long-spined black variety, but it is equally as dangerous. As if to lure the unwary, it appears to be a globe of numerous tiny flowers. It is so colorful it invites the skin diver to pick it up.

Except for the trained collector with the proper grasping tools, it should only be observed and perhaps photographed. To touch it with the bare hand is to become envenomated with a powerful poison.

When magnified, this dome of "flowers" will appear as little trumpets, with the bells in the shape of triangles. On the corner of each of these points are tiny fangs called pedicellariae. When touched, the three corners close, driving the clawlike fangs into the flesh. The stabs of pain will cause the victim to withdraw quickly, but the pedicellariae have not finished their work. They will immediately break free of the urchin, as they continue to exude venom long after they have been dislodged.

Although many of the poisonous species of sea urchins have developed venom of different properties, the medical aspects are similar. The initial contact produces sharp pain, much like being stung by bees. It is followed by an aching sensation and a reddening and swelling of the flesh. Within minutes there is usually a feeling of faintness and muscular paralysis. Respiratory distress is not uncommon and the paralysis may continue for hours after the stabbing pain has subsided.

Human death from sea urchins is rare, but cannot be entirely dismissed, since cases have been reported. Much depends on the severity of the contact and the individual's tolerance to certain types of poison. The average human finds the sting of bees and similar insects only painful; for others it can be fatal.

In various parts of the world the eggs of sea urchins are eaten by people who have developed a taste for them. Depending on the species and the region, the eggs are eaten in different ways. In some cases the spines are scraped away and the egg mass inside the urchin shell is eaten raw with a sprinkle of lemon or lime juice. Other connoisseurs prefer them combined with hen eggs and cooked by scrambling. The taste is not unlike the edible roe of many types of fish.

Starfish

Like sea urchins, starfish are echinoderms and there are numerous species. Almost all are harmless and may be handled freely. From a commercial standpoint, starfish are decidedly objectionable because of their widespread destruction of valuable shellfish such as oysters and clams.

There is one species, however, that causes trouble in two ways. It is known as the Crown-of-thorns, *Acanthaster planci*. It has recently been observed to be increasing in numbers and some investigators have expressed concern over the eventual fate of Australia's Great Barrier Reef because of this starfish.

The Crown-of-thorns is quite large, with a spread of nearly two feet. Some have twelve or more "legs" and it is believed to cause extensive destruction by feeding on the new growth of coral. It is a beautiful star with brilliant red and snow white markings and is covered with a prickly armor of sharp spines.

Each of these spines contains a painful venom in the covering sheath. If stepped on or carelessly handled, the spines will puncture flesh in numerous places at once. The symptoms are much the same as those of the black sea urchin. Because of its size and vivid color pattern, however, it is easily avoided.

Giant Clams

When the writer of horror stories, who specializes in having the hero encounter all manner of underwater perils, has exhausted all of the standard demons, he eventually turns to the "man-eating clam." Of course, there is no such creature, but the giant clam, *Tridacna gigas*, of the phylum Mollusca, is frequently referred to as an eater of men.

The standard yarn usually has a South Pacific setting and the victim is often diving for pearl oysters or sunken treasure. As the story unfolds the expendable character is grasped by a foot or hand by the sinister bivalve. There follows a valiant struggle as the hero attempts to free his companion. It is usually a futile effort and the hapless diver is abandoned. The desired impression is that as soon as the victim ceases moving the clam will draw him into its cavernous shell and digest him.

Such a sequence was ideal for producers of B-grade movies. It gave the underwater photographer a chance to demonstrate his skill at showing all manner of surrounding sea life without having to keep track of a fast-moving shark. Nor did the "special effects" crew have to make an artificial octopus look reasonably realistic. The audience sat on the edge of their seats and all but held their collective breath until the trial was over.

With the passage of time moviegoers became more sophisticated and refused to be hoodwinked by such hocum. Creeping and crawling creatures with a highly advanced knowledge of space travel might come to earth from the planet Mars, but who would be so naive as to believe a man could be captured by a clam?

It might be of interest, however, to have a look at the shells of a giant clam on the next visit to a marine aquarium. The shells may measure four feet from one end to the other and are fluted at the top so that when closed they interlock. In life it is hinged along the bottom and filled with an oysterlike animal. It is so heavy that it would require the skill and strength of several men working with block and tackle to dislodge it from the bottom and haul it to the surface.

As it grows it usually becomes partially imbedded in sand and coral. It may be resting just below the surface or in water twenty-five feet deep. When living it is coated with greenish-brown algae and when not disturbed the slimy mantle extends slightly above the scalloped edge, feeding constantly on algae and drifting plankton.

The only means of defense are the ponderously thick shells and powerful adductor muscles. If a careless fish or crab makes the mistake of touching the sensitive mantle, it is instantly sucked into the shells and the muscles contract. If they could be wedged so that the shells were agape, it would still exert such pressure as to resist the leverage of a large crowbar that might be used in an attempt to pry them apart.

For a moment you might draw on your imagination and

picture yourself as a skin diver exploring a reef. As you look about through your faceplate something attracts your attention. You reach out for the reef to shove away in a different direction. Instead of pushing against solid coral, your hand slips into the gooey mantle of a giant clam. Before you have time to realize what has happened, the powerful adductor muscles have reacted and the rock-hard jaws are holding you with the tenacity of a bear trap.

If you have scuba tanks strapped to your back, time is on your side. If you are wearing only a mask and flippers, you may have a full two minutes before you run out of air. The clam will complacently stay locked until its sensory organs detect there is no longer any danger, because all movement has stopped. At that time the mantle will reemerge and continue feeding on algae. For what consolation it may be, you will not be eaten by a clam. Your lifeless body will simply drift away and possibly provide a free meal for a foraging shark or a collection of crabs.

Admittedly, such a macabre event is quite remote for three main reasons. One is that such large clams are comparatively rare; two, because a skin diver would have little trouble in spotting the bright color of the wavy mantle—which may be blue, green, or red—its distinct shape and color should offer ample warning to steer clear; finally, the mantle of the giant clam is so sensitive it would normally cause the shells to close before any large object could enter. But, it is possible.

Since such clams are occasionally found in water shallow enough for wading, the chances are more likely that an incautious foot might be clamped in the same manner. In such an event, it would be necessary to dig down into this giant bivalve with a sharp knife the size of a large machete and sever the two adductor muscles. Once this is done the tension is automatically released and a hand or foot could be withdrawn.

Because the clam must have sunlight to produce its food, it is not a creature that might be encountered in a dark underwater cavern, or below the range of sunlit waters.

Cone Shells

It is true that giant clams have caused human drownings, but in the world of seashells there is one that is a decidedly greater threat. Far more numerous, more sought after, and small enough to be held in the palm of the hand is the cone shell of the genus Conus. Some species possess a deadly poisonous dart that can and has killed those who have failed to exercise caution in handling them while they are still alive.

There are at least four hundred species of cones. They are found in tropical seas around the world and some are so prized by conchologists as to demand prices in excess of a thousand dollars for a single specimen. For example, the Glory-of-the-Seas, *Conus gloria-maris,* is rated as one of the rarest and, because of its scarcity and beauty, is considered the most valuable. Another rare, beautiful, and deadly one is the Geographer cone, *Conus geographus.*

As is so often the case where many dangerous sea creatures are concerned, the Indo-Pacific is the home of the most dangerous cones. The venom apparatus is in the form of a dart tucked inside the cone's cavity and resembles a miniature harpoon, with shaft and barbed point. This is connected to a ligament gland attached to a venom gland or duct inside the shell. At least two cones, the Chinese alphabet cone, *C. spurius,* and the Queen cone, *C. regius,* are found in the Caribbean. Investigation is incomplete, but both are suspected of being dangerous.

The cone's food, which is hunted primarily at night, consists of various forms of sea life, including very small fish. Since the prey is so small, its highly dangerous poison is one of the baffling peculiarities of nature. Why, one may logically ask, do some have venom strong enough to kill a creature as large as a human, while others are harmless? This is even more puzzling when it is realized that the food they depend on is much the same. It is as unanswerable as an attempt to

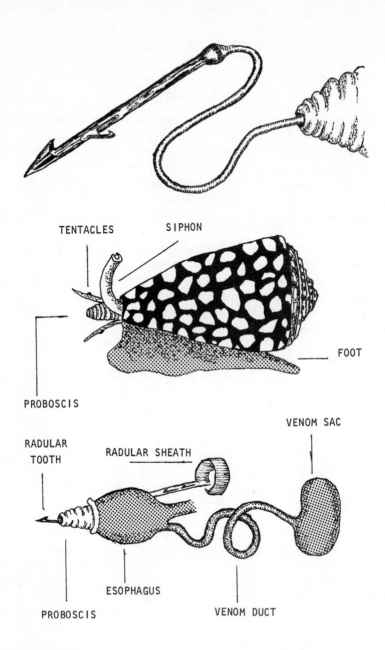

TENTACLES SIPHON

PROBOSCIS

FOOT

VENOM SAC

RADULAR TOOTH RADULAR SHEATH

PROBOSCIS ESOPHAGUS VENOM DUCT

Drawing of cone shell.

explain why a black widow spider is so dangerous, while countless other spiders are as harmless to humans as a common butterfly. Such is so, however, and to grasp a cone sliding along the bottom or resting in a small shelter is a dangerous practice.

The instant a dangerous cone becomes aware it is captured, the harpoon is ejected from the open end of the shell and will penetrate the flesh as easily as a sharp needle. The chemical formula of the venom is not fully understood, except that it has a paralytic effect on both heart and lungs.

When moving about in search of worms and other forms of food the cone's shell is almost completely covered by the extended mantle. It is often so covered as to resemble nothing more than a small glob of living flesh. At rest, with the mantle withdrawn, even an amateur collector would recognize it as a prize find.

It makes little difference to the cone whether it is hunting or at rest; if it is incautiously handled the venomous harpoon is launched and the damage is done in a fleeting second. The safest method to collect any cone that may possibly be dangerous is to scoop it up with an aquarium net and place it in a suitable container. Later, the creature can be killed by placing it in boiling water, after which it can be withdrawn from the shell with a pair of pointed pliers.

If contact is made with a dangerous species the initial symptoms begin with a burning sting at the point where the dart has entered the flesh. A numbness follows quickly and is often accompanied by a tingling sensation that begins to spread over the entire body, most noticeable in the mouth and on the lips.

If the cone that has caused the injury is of a highly dangerous species the next symptom is a general paralysis. The victim may lapse into a coma and if medical aid is not soon available the person may die. Under any conditions the primary concern should be to get the victim to a hospital as quickly as possible. Since the venom has not been isolated, the treatment will be to cope with the individual symptoms as they develop.

Worms

There are many different types of worms found in salt water and most of them are completely harmless to humans. There are a few types, however, that can cause trouble. One of these is the flatworm of the phylum Platyhelminthes, commonly known as "swimmer's itch." These should not be confused with the freshwater flatworms, *Schistosomiasis,* which are decidedly more dangerous because they invade the liver, intestines, and other organs.

The marine flatworm is found in temperate and subtropical salt waters, showing up from time to time at isolated spots along the coast. When it does appear, it is generally in vast numbers and may be present for several months at a time. After a period of annoyance, it may suddenly vanish and not be detected in the same area for many years. The larval stage penetrates the skin in considerable numbers in areas of high infestation. Its presence is noticeable as small pimples that cause distress in the form of a persistent itch.

Once noticed it is wise to avoid further swimming and wash thoroughly, then sponge the body with a diluted solution of ammonia and water. If the papules have not begun to vanish on the following day a physician should be consulted. With the use of ointments, such as those containing cortisone, the irritation can be eliminated completely in about two days.

The life cycle of marine flatworms is complex. In its early stages of development it is found first in certain saltwater snails. These, in turn, are eaten by various sea birds and the worm remains in the intestinal tract until it is emptied into the water. From that point it remains free-swimming until it can burrow into living flesh.

The bristleworm is a segmented worm of the phylum Annelida. One species, *Eurythoe complanata,* is found throughout the Caribbean, the warm waters of the Pacific, and the Gulf of Mexico. Also in the Gulf is a similar species, *Hermodice carunculata.*

Full-grown specimens measure a foot or more in length and resemble some of the woolly caterpillars, except that they are much larger. Most species are green in color and some have red markings. The bristles are generally dull white, tipped with a rust red color. The bristles normally lie flat along the worm's body, but are instantly erected when touched.

Some species occasionally swim on the surface while others are confined to the bottom. The bottom dwellers may be found creeping about among rocks and in coral formations. Infrequently they will attach themselves to baited hooks and be brought to the surface in this manner.

Touching or brushing against any of these worms will cause an intense stinging as the bristles penetrate the flesh. The pain will continue until the bristles are removed and, even then, local swelling and a feeling of numbness may be expected. In some cases the irritation subsides in a matter of a few hours, while in others it may continue for as long as two days.

Picking the fine bristles out with tweezers is a tedious process. Removal can be accomplished faster and more effectively if the flesh is covered by adhesive tape. The tape is then pulled off quickly and the poisonous setae are drawn with it. Diluted ammonia or rubbing alcohol will cause the pain to subside. The effects of bristleworm stings are not serious, but they are usually painful. No attempt should be made to handle them unless rubber gloves are worn.

Because of their particular attraction to numerous species of game fishes, livebait anglers often use bloodworms. Those most numerous along the east coast of North America are found from the Bay of Fundy south to the Carolinas. The two most frequently collected for bait are *Glycera americana* and *Glycera dibranchiata*. Specimens ten inches in length are not uncommon and some occasionally reach a length of two feet. They are easily identified by their reddish color and rows of small "legs" that extend along the length of the body on both sides.

Bloodworms are found in shallow flats under stones and around clumps of seaweed. They have a circular mouth with tiny sharp teeth that can bite human flesh. Because of the worm's sluggish nature, few fishermen are bitten and those who are, not usually bothered. There are those, however, who are allergic and report the bite to be as painful as a bee sting.

Individuals who are sensitive will feel the pain immediately and notice a blanching of the skin around the bite. The flesh becomes hot and slightly swollen. It is simply a bite and there is no sting to be removed. There may be a slight itching sensation that will persist for a day or so. This can often be avoided if a mild antiseptic is applied quickly. No further treatment is necessary.

3

Morays

One of the oddest and probably most misunderstood of the dangerous creatures that inhabit tropical and subtropical salt waters around the world is the moray, of the family Muraenidae. It is frequently referred to as the moray eel and, although it resembles an eel in appearance, is not a true eel.

American and European varieties of true eels are catadromous in nature in that they hatch in the sea and travel up freshwater streams to lakes and ponds where they spend the majority of their lives. As their life-span nears completion, the female begins the long journey back to the sea where both sexes mate. The female then continues far out into the Atlantic to her place of origin, spawns, and dies.

Morays, however, are strictly saltwater creatures and, although there are over a hundred species scattered about the world, it is believed each type spends its entire life in the general vicinity in which it originated.

One of the most popular beliefs is that the moray possesses venomous fangs and is as deadly as the cobras and certain sea snakes. This is not so, but it does not prevent them from being listed as a decidedly dangerous sea creature. Paradoxically, people have died as a result of the bite of a moray and there is still another way this creature can cause human death. This is by the human consumption of its flesh which is occasionally poisonous.

Brown moray.

Of the numerous species, the common green moray, *Gym-nothorax funebris,* frequently encountered in the warm At-lantic, Caribbean, and Gulf of Mexico, is among the largest. It reaches a length of six to ten feet and may be as thick as a man's thigh. It has relatives of equal size in other parts of the world. The brown moray, *Enchelynassa canina,* of the Pacific equals the green in size and a weight of seventy-five pounds is not unusual.

Although differing in color, marking, and size, all morays are much alike in general characteristics. Unlike most true fish, they lack scales. Their thick skin, which is coated with a slimy mucus, provides ample protection. In many species the head is large and the powerful jaws are pointed and studded with needle-sharp teeth that frequently measure over an inch in length. They lack the pectoral and pelvic fins, common to true fish, and the gill openings are reduced to small rounded holes.

When necessary they are able to swim, but they prefer to spend most of their time in reef crevices, around rock piles, the debris of wrecks, and the jumble of litter often found at the base of bridge abutments. Any place that affords reasonably permanent shelter is likely to be home for the moray. Here, it can rest or glide about in snakelike fashion as it searches for food.

It is because of the length of the teeth and powerful jaws, combined with a pugnacious temperament, that humans may be seriously injured. The teeth, invariably contaminated, are driven deeply into flesh, and unless proper medical aid is available a serious infection of a tetanus nature is almost certain to result. It is this fact that has led many to believe that the moray has venomous fangs.

Many fishing boat skippers and men who make their living on the sea will not permit a moray to be brought aboard. Under normal circumstances, they are justified in their cau-

Green moray.

Two green morays in rocks.

tion, because in or out of the water, the moray is a vicious creature and will snap at anything that moves within range.

They are frequently hooked by fishermen, but only rarely is a large one landed. The exception comes when one is hooked while away from its lair. They have none of the fighting qualities of a game fish and it is simply a matter of lifting the weight from the bottom. If, however, they grab the baited hook while on home base, they will lodge themselves in some underwater obstruction and be securely anchored. Then it is a question whether the line breaks or the hook is ripped out of their mouths, but seldom will they allow themselves to be pulled out of their labyrinthine sanctuary.

Still, a percentage are hooked in open water and it is after one is brought aboard that incautious anglers are often injured. Many people are curious and want to examine what they have boated, no matter how repulsive it may appear. Such inquisitiveness is commendable and there is no question that the store of scientific knowledge is increased by this form of field study. But, where a moray is the subject, the investigator had better know what he is doing and proceed with caution.

If it is decided that the catch is not worth keeping, many anglers feel it is their duty to remove the hook before tossing the creature back over the side. It requires only one unpleasant encounter with a hooked moray to convince the fisherman that the task is not worth the risk.

Moray, swimming.

Where the average fish is concerned, a pair of metal grippers, a fish mitt, or even bare hands are all that may be required to remove a hook. This, however, is seldom the case where a moray is concerned. Just the simple act of getting a secure grip on one is a hazardous feat because of their agility and the thick coating of slime. Those skilled in handling true eels will quickly discover they have an entirely different creature to contend with in the form of a moray. For that matter, leaving a hook in the jaw of any fish, the moray included, is not nearly as brutal an act as some believe. It will soon rust out and, even before it does, the fish will resume feeding.

One persistent bit of folklore is that these creatures, especially large ones, will grasp a human swimmer and hold him beneath the surface until he drowns. Those who relate such imaginative tales will explain that the moray grasps the victim with its jaws and then wraps several coils around the body in the manner of a boa, anaconda, or python. One skin diver reported such an encounter, explaining that he was able to free himself because he was especially adept at holding his breath for an abnormal length of time and that while he was trapped he repeatedly stabbed the moray with his sheath knife until the creature expired.

It is a decidedly unlikely story for two distinct reasons. First, despite its many unpleasant aspects, the moray is not a constrictor and secondly, it is not the nature of the moray to keep its jaws locked shut for an extended period. Rather, it will bite savagely, turn loose, and bite again. In the manner of fishes, it must depend on opening and closing its jaws at somewhat regular intervals in order to keep a flow of water passing over its gills. In all fairness to the skin diver, however, it must be admitted that the moray can, if the need arises, keep its jaws closed much longer than the average fish.

In all probability the belief that the moray is a constrictor has gained credulousness by watching a specimen that has been hooked and hauled ashore or into a boat. They have a peculiar habit when in trouble of tying their body into an overhand knot and at such times they will exert considerable pressure, but it is not a motionless grip. When indulging in such contortions they will draw the knot tight and swiftly withdraw the anterior portion. At times the pressure will be so great that the stomach contents are expelled from the mouth.

The entire performance is executed swiftly and brought to a standstill only if the movement is impeded by a spear that has been driven completely through the body. If a hook is in the jaw the length of the moray's knotted body will continue on up the leader. When the stunt is rapidly repeated the line and leader quickly become tangled and covered in slime. For an untrained observer witnessing the pressure exerted during this knot-tying by even a small moray, little imagination is required to speculate on what the outcome would be if a human body were caught in the coil of one that measures ten feet in length.

The habit of tying themselves in a knot and quickly withdrawing the head quite likely stems from a practice they employ with octopuses. These cephalopods, especially small ones, are an important part of the moray's diet. When they grab an octopus the creature will try to avoid being eaten by endeavoring to attach one or more sucker-studded arms around the moray's body. To free itself quickly, the moray forms its overhand knot and as the head is retracted through the loop, the arms are swept off.

After Thor Heyerdahl and his fellow crew members of the *Kon-Tiki* had traveled over four thousand miles across the Pacific and wrecked on the reef in the Tuamotu Archipelago they had an unpleasant encounter with morays. Two of the modern explorers reported being attacked by a total of eight morays. They stated that the creatures were as large around as the calf of a man's leg and were speckled with green and black spots. (Probably of the *Enchelynassa canina* species.) They managed to escape injury by scrambling up on exposed coral hillocks and discouraged further molestation by killing two of the creatures with machetes.

Some years ago while spearfishing along a reef in a small bay in the Hawaiian Islands, I had a confrontation with a moray that I would not like to have again. Aside from a spear, my only underwater equipment consisted of a pair of rustic goggles. Without even a snorkel tube, I spent most of my time rising to the surface for air and diving back down again.

The fish life was plentiful, but I had been unable to spear one until about the seventh dive. The species was unknown to me and all I was able to see was that it was dull silver over most of the body with distinct vertical marks near the head. I was at the surface when it wriggled free. Taking a quick breath, I dived again, hoping to catch sight of it before it vanished in the bottom growth. As I stroked downward I saw it disappear in an opening in one of the coral heads. When I reached the spot I could not see where it had gone, so once again, I returned to the surface, leaving my spear below to mark the spot.

After a brief period of floating on my back and resting, I readjusted my goggles and dived again. Quickly locating my spear, I began to search the crevice where I thought I had last seen it. There was something inside and I thought I detected a slight movement. Determined to regain my prize, I eased the spear into the hole and gave it a strong thrust.

There was no doubt that I had struck some living creature. The long handle of the spear was wrested from my grasp and it began to gyrate to such an extent that I was forced to back away to avoid being struck by the shaft. Another trip to the surface and an almost immediate dive showed the spear was still whipping about. I caught it and attempted to pull it out, but with no success. By then I began to believe the tip might be imbedded in the arm of an octopus.

I had caught several of these on previous hunting trips and was convinced I was going to have a struggle drawing the creature out because it was holding fast in the honeycomb of the coral. I reasoned that if I exerted enough of a pull on the spear handle the barbed end would eventually be ripped out. Accordingly, I braced my feet against the coral and began to pull. It seemed to be lodged as securely as King Arthur's Excalibur, or, more prosaically, as if I had hammered it into a rubber tire.

After a minute or so had passed I realized I was going to be forced to return again to the surface. During a pause of several seconds I looked upward through the clear water. Just above my head and a bit to the left I saw the head of a moray and about two feet of the neck protruding from another hole. The creature was arched over and its tooth-studded mouth was snapping at me.

Shoving myself away from the reef I made a swift trip to the surface. As I regained my breath I began to realize what had happened. I had driven the spear into some portion of the moray's body. There was no way to be certain how far back, but that was why the spear shaft was twisting and jerking about. The moray was obviously in some sort of coral tunnel and the spear was so deeply imbedded in the muscular body that it could not pull the spear along behind as it attempted to emerge from the upper opening.

After a moment or so I dived again. This time I could see the spear pointed rigidly toward the bottom and as I examined the situation I realized more of the moray's body was protruding from the upper portion of the little tunnel. For a fleeting moment I considered continuing to attempt to retrieve my spear. Suddenly, I realized what a stupid mistake that would be. The injured creature was in a vicious mood and if I did manage to pull the spear free, it would automatically free the dangerous moray. From the way it was lashing from side to side, I knew the instant it broke loose it would attack.

It was a new spear and I disliked leaving it, but when the full import of the situation was apparent I knew my only sensible course of action was to depart immediately. With all of the force I had exerted it might, even at that moment, have been only a fraction of an inch from breaking through the tough hide. The cost of the spear suddenly counted for nothing and I stroked swiftly for the surface, pushed the goggles back on my head, and swam for my outrigger canoe, desperately hoping the spear would hold the moray long enough to allow me to get into the boat.

How close I had come to a serious encounter could only be a matter of conjecture. As I sat in the canoe and pondered the event I tried to imagine the size of the animal I had unwittingly speared. That, too, was something at which I could only guess. I had seen the head at close range and knew it was as wide as my hand. There was no way to accurately estimate the length of the body, because there was no way of knowing whether the spear had entered halfway along the length or near the tail. Considering the size of the head and the two feet of neck that was protruding and adding that to the distance down to my spear, I was convinced the creature was at least six feet long.

There have been no verified accounts of swimmers being attacked by morays along North American beaches, probably because they seldom venture into areas frequented by these creatures. Skin divers occasionally put themselves in positions where attacks are more likely to occur. Even then, attacks can generally be classified as provoked attacks, just as mine would have had to have been rated if the moray had broken free while I was still nearby.

One frightful example of an unprovoked attack on a skin diver is reported by A. J. McClane in his *Fishing Encyclopedia* (Holt, Rinehart and Winston, 1965). This was a vicious attack which occurred in 1961 near Key West, Florida. The spearfisherman was Lieutenant Rudy Enders who was an instructor at the Navy Underwater Swimming School. According to McClane, Enders was searching for fish in thirty feet of water and had not found any to his liking. As he was rising to the surface for air he passed a ledge where a green moray, *Gymnothorax funebris*, lashed out at him from a hole and grabbed his right wrist, delivering such a severe bite that Enders was hospitalized for several weeks.

This account had an odd sequel and may or may not have involved the same moray. Several months later Enders and a companion, Scott Slaughter, were again diving in the same location. This time a moray that Slaughter reported as being at least seven feet long poured out of its hiding place and was about to strike Enders on the neck. To the young lieutenant's good fortune, Slaughter shot a spear into the creature's head. It pulled free, however, and disappeared in the rocks.

Many fishermen fish not only for the sport but they will frequently cook and eat almost anything they catch. A large number of anglers deliberately fish for eels in fresh water, having found them to be excellent tablefare when properly prepared. It logically follows that when some of these fishermen are on salt water and successfully subdue a moray, they look on it as an eel and take it home for the frying pan. They may be lucky and dine on moray flesh time after time. Eventually, the law of averages is almost certain to catch up with them and they could be severely poisoned—so severely that it may be the last meal they and their dining companions will ever eat.

The facts are that not all morays, even of the same species, are poisonous to eat, nor is the individual specimen always poisonous. It depends largely on what type of fish they have been feeding upon. As commendable as it may be not to waste food, it borders on sheer folly to chance eating one that all too often has highly toxic flesh.

There are several theories as to why one specimen has this dangerous toxin in its flesh and others of the same species do not. Certain types of fishes, particularly members of the puffer group, are known to always contain a high concentration of dangerous toxin in their internal organs. The most widely accepted theory is that occasionally one particular moray will feed extensively on these fish over a period of time. The toxin

Puffer.

apparently does not adversely affect the moray, but the poison is absorbed in its flesh and is carried on to the humans who eat it. It should be emphasized that cooking does not destroy this type of toxin.

Those who have experienced the misfortune of dining on poisonous moray flesh report the initial symptoms begin with a tingling and numbing sensation about the lips and tongue. This quickly spreads to the hands and feet and with it comes a feeling of excessive weight of the arms and legs. Depending upon the severity of the poisoning, there may be additional discomfort in the form of diarrhea, abdominal pains, and aching of the joints of the body. Other symptoms include nausea, vomiting, difficulty in swallowing, and constriction of the respiratory system.

As with most sea creatures, morays will generally try to escape before biting. They are, however, somewhat more pugnacious and unpredictable than many other sea animals. They could not utilize man as food in any way and when they do bite it is usually because they have been molested, or feel their safety is threatened. In cases where several have been known to attack, it may be assumed they were breeding or spawning and are simply trying to drive away any intruder.

Except under abnormal conditions they will not come to the surface and are seldom found in water where there is not adequate bottom coverage to provide concealment. Spearing them is a dangerous practice, because they are likely to twist free. The chance of killing or disabling one with a spear is remote and it may cause them to attack.

The treatment for the bite of a moray is much the same as for any other skin puncture. Logically, the deeper the penetration of the teeth, the more dangerous the wound. As a first-aid measure, bleeding from the bitten area should be encouraged and antiseptic should be used. Because the teeth of many morays are needle-sharp and the jaws are powerful, it is well to suspect the punctures may be deeper than they appear. Because of the contaminated teeth, the victim should have the wound examined by a physician.

4

Teeth, Spines, and Venom

When one spends a goodly portion of his time on and near salt water over a number of years and under a wide variety of conditions it is almost certain that he will, at one time or another, find himself in the company of fishermen from all walks of life. There will be the sporting anglers, many of whom set their sights on a selected few types of fishes and virtually ignore most others. There will be charterboat captains who earn their livelihood by taking other people fishing. Then there will be the average fishermen who just like to fish and go out after whatever they can catch. Some will be newcomers, some old-timers, and there is a growing number who find their sport by hunting with a spear. Not to be overlooked are the commercial fishermen who lead a rough life with nets, hand lines, boats, and all kinds of weather.

One goal they all have in common is that they are in quest of fish. One of the most popular beliefs held by the nonfisherman is that those who do fish are either inveterate liars or, at best, prone to gross exaggeration. The classic example is how "the big one that got away" continues to grow each time the story is repeated. Also, there are those who return home with some seemingly fanciful tale about an odd sighting or how they saw a fish do something that is too preposterous to be readily believed by even another fisherman.

Net fishermen.

Some years ago I was fishing with a man who had spent much of his life as a commercial fisherman. Eventually the subject of sharks entered the conversation and we discussed their potential danger at some length. The man related a few close calls he had experienced with them and told of others he knew to be true. He startled me when he suddenly stood up, removed his shirt, and lowered his pants. When his divestment was nearly absolute he began pointing to numerous small scars on his arms, legs, and torso. It did not require the trained eye of a physician to look at the scars and guess they had originally been moderately severe wounds.

For a while he insisted that I try to guess what had caused them. I was at a loss for any logical suspicion. They ranged in size from less than an inch to several that were at least two inches long. At his insistence I made a few guesses that included shrapnel wounds, or maybe he had been caught in a barbed wire entanglement, or perhaps tumbled down a rocky hillside.

"You're not even close," he said. "If it had been anything like that there would be scars on my face and head, wouldn't there?"

I nodded in agreement as he replaced his clothing. "You ain't gonna believe this, but I got all them scars early one morning when me and two others made a strike on a school of big Spanish mackerel. Happened right over yonder near that little island," he said, nodding over his shoulder toward the coastline. "I got cut up so bad they had to leave the net and get me to a hospital. Them doctors had to do an awful lot of sewing and they even had to give me one of them blood transfusions."

Here, I thought, was a fish tale that could win any liar's contest that might be held by fishermen. I had caught countless Spanish mackerel, *Scomberomorus maculatus,* and, admittedly, I had been nipped a few times while removing lures from the mouths of boated fish, but certainly nothing serious. Continuing, the man told how he and those with him had surrounded a school of mackerel and as they were attempting to drag the two ends of the seine toward the beach,

Fish nomenclature.

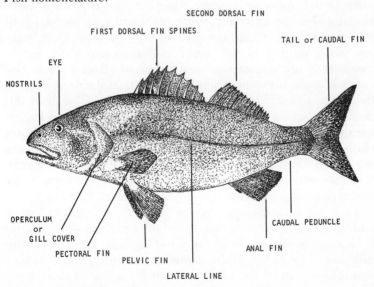

it became snagged on some underwater obstruction. According to his story, he had rowed out to the trouble spot and dived overboard to free the lead line.

He said the moment he dove into the water the trapped mackerel began to hit him with vicious bites and in the confusion the boat drifted away and he had to swim back to the beach. By the time he was ashore he had been bitten well over thirty times. It was his story and, while I did not believe it, I tried to express the proper amount of interest, but I kept my thoughts to myself. The trouble was I simply had not become acquainted with enough commercial fishermen who worked in the days when haul seines were legal in Florida coastal waters.

Since that time I have heard numerous similar fish stories from other commercial fishermen to convince me that my old friend was indeed telling the truth. Apparently such behavior is not common, but such incidents have occurred from time to time. Most of those who have told such tales have emphasized that the mackerel were large and in a frenzy at finding so many of their number confined in a net.

Since fish are wild creatures they can be expected to occasionally react in an atypical manner when they are trapped, still in good health, and not prohibited from swimming. Anyone who has fished for bluefish, *Pomatomus saltatrix*, is aware they are one of the most active of all game fish. Because of their voracious appetite they attack shoals of smaller fish with a fury that has gained them the title "wolf of the sea." They are well distributed around the world and fishermen know they can inflict painful bites to human flesh, especially when just caught. What is not generally known is that a school of large ones—those ranging from ten to twenty pounds—will actually attack human swimmers if a ravenous group moves into waters where people are surf bathing.

Such an occurrence is rare and must be triggered by a combination of circumstances, all in progress at the same time. Among these may be the set of the tide, wind direction, migration of bluefish in the immediate vicinity, roiled bottom conditions, and an abundance of bait fish close to shore.

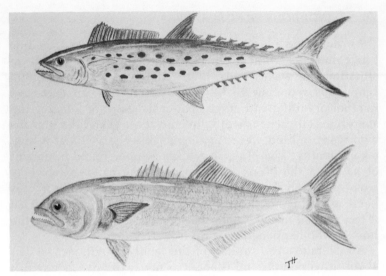

Spanish mackerel (top) and bluefish.

Such were the conditions on April 12, 1974, along the beaches near Miami, Florida. Swimmers were driven from the Atlantic waters in droves by countless numbers of large bluefish that were excitedly feeding on smaller fish in the surf. Because the event was abnormal and so many people were injured, the episode received extensive press coverage. Lifeguards, with years of experience in the area, stated they had never seen such frantic confusion involving so many people and fish. Many of the injuries consisted of simple painful bites and gashes while others were of a more serious nature. One swimmer's finger was almost severed, another came near losing a thumb, while another was so viciously bitten on the heel that several dozen stitches were necessary to close the wound.

The excitement began about 8:30 A.M. and centered along a stretch of beach known as Bakers Haulover. At first sharks or barracuda were suspected, but experienced fishermen identified the culprits as bluefish. As a safety measure the beaches were temporarily closed until the majority of the voracious fish had departed.

As vicious as bluefish can be when they are on a feeding binge, humans are never included in their diet. In the above situation the waves were high enough to roil the bottom sand, thus reducing visibility. Added to this, an excessive number of mullet and other smaller fishes were hugging the shoreline. The attacks were directed at these and the humans who were injured were unquestionably the victims of mistaken identity. The bluefish is a fast swimmer, and in pursuit of its target the blurred sight of a human hand or foot may have suggested a small fish. When the competition for food is keen, as in this case, the bluefish bores in for the attack. That it has made a mistake does not lessen the injury done to the human who happened to be in its path.

An average-sized mullet, of the family Mugilidae, weighs about three pounds and is about as nonaggressive as any fish that swims. Its diet consists mainly of minute forms of animal and plant life sucked up by a small mouth. They generally travel in schools that may number anywhere from a dozen to several hundred. At times they move in large shoals, with thousands passing a given point in a matter of hours.

Like many other fishes, mullet will frequently jump well out of the water. They indulge in this jumping habit both day and night and no one has ever proven positively why. Often a boat, such as an open skiff with a bright light, such as a lantern, showing will cause them to begin jumping and it is a common occurrence for them to land in the boat. Also undetermined is whether they are jumping toward the light or whether they become frightened and jump in whichever direction they happen to be swimming.

It matters little why they jump, but to suddenly and unexpectedly have a very lively fish bouncing about over the bottom boards seldom fails to startle the human occupants. Occasionally one of these decidedly inoffensive fish has been known to send a nocturnal fisherman back home with a black eye. Such is always a joke to everyone except the hapless victim who not only has to suffer the minor pain and temporary disfigurement but also has to explain that the wallop was delivered by a mullet. He is generally subjected to the same suspicious comments as is the person who honestly reports that he received his black eye by running into a partially opened door while moving from one darkened room to another.

It seems implausible until one stops to consider the speed at which a fish of several pounds must generate before it hurls itself into the air in a jump that can cover a distance of several feet. The weight of the fish combined with the speed closely approximate a solid blow from a clinched fist. The odds are much in favor of the mullet simply landing in the boat, less that it will strike an occupant, and still more remote that it will hit a vulnerable spot on the human anatomy. Nevertheless, it has happened often enough to be part of the repertoire of many fishermen's stores of unusual fish stories.

Even more preposterous is an account of an episode which actually happened to three commercial mullet fishermen operating out of a small town on the northern shore of the Gulf of Mexico. To make the flat statement that the three hard-working men had to engage in a frantic struggle to prevent one of their boats from being sunk by mullet is almost more than even the most gullible listener is willing to accept. Yet, the fishermen have stuck to their original story over the intervening years and because of its unusual aspects it is worth repeating while on the subject of unusual fish behavior.

The three were net fishermen, and to properly spread their gill nets and make the trips profitable, they used two open boats. One was a twelve-foot skiff and the other was a seventeen-footer. The larger boat was used to carry the long net and was equipped with a small outboard motor and a bare, battery-powered light bulb suspended from a stubby mast stepped near the midsection. The light was necessary because the fishermen frequently worked at night when tidal conditions called for it. The smaller and more maneuverable skiff was used to aid in collecting the fish that had become trapped in the mesh of the net.

On the night in question the three had made an average haul and, with the smaller boat in tow, had started the out-

School of mullet.

board and were returning home. As they moved along across the smooth water they were engaged in their standard practice of cleaning as many of the fish as possible, to more profitably utilize the time. In order to see what they were doing, they followed their customary procedure of connecting the "working light" on the mast.

Everything was seemingly normal and they took little notice when a mullet jumped into the boat, followed by another and one that hit the gunwale and bounced back into the water. Such things happened almost every time they fished at night. In a matter of minutes, however, a decidedly unusual situation began developing. As they were calmly working at their chore and moving along over the water, they were unaware that the outboard motor was driving them into a shoal of surface swimming mullet that may have numbered well into the thousands.

Even as many mullet began leaping and splashing all around them they simply assumed they were passing through a small school. When a dozen or so had landed inside they were pleased that their nightly catch was being increased. When the number tripled and quadrupled they were even more delighted.

By the time ten minutes had passed and the jumping mullet had increased and the activity showed no sign of diminishing, they became mildly concerned that their boat might possibly become overloaded. They shut off the outboard and pulled the skiff alongside. It was already loaded with part of the catch, but there was still room for more, so they started pitching extra fish into it. As they drew it closer to the circle of light they noticed that some of the jumping mullet began landing in the smaller boat just as in the larger. In short order it became apparent that the number of "free" fish was going to exceed what they considered a safe load and they began tossing mullet back over the side.

The outboard was restarted and they opened the throttle wide in an effort to break free of the excited fish. Instead of relief, they found the situation was becoming more critical. They already had more mullet aboard than they would normally have expected to catch in three profitable trips. The larger boat was so loaded that they had dangerously little freeboard left and it became necessary to move with caution to avoid taking water over the gunwales. It was by then obvious that if they could not quickly move out of the concentration they were definitely in danger of swamping.

Although the storage battery was by then completely covered with flopping fish, one of the men grabbed the wires and snatched them from the terminals. Almost immediately the fish stopped jumping aboard, but because of the excessive weight the straining outboard was able to push them shoreward at a decidedly reduced speed.

By the time they eventually tied up at the fish house pier and unloaded their catch, the sun was beginning to rise and the owner of the fish house, along with a couple of workmen, had arrived. When they saw the numerous wire baskets filled with freshly caught fish they were convinced that several other boats had stopped off to unload. It was not until no one came to claim and be paid for their share that those along the waterfront began to believe the story told by the bewildered fishermen.

All knew the three were seamen with sufficient experience not to intentionally overload their boats beyond the danger point. The question of the light was debated for some time. It may have been coincidental that just as the light was extinguished the fishermen passed out of the concentration of fish. There are at least three men, however, who will never believe that mullet do not jump *toward* a light, instead of simply jumping when a light appears.

In discussing the event, all three confessed that their greatest fear was not that they would sink. That within itself would have been serious, but what each had more concern about was that the excess amount of partially disabled and already dead fish would have attracted sharks. It was a sobering thought, especially when one considers how sharks frequently go into a feeding frenzy when an abundance of food is suddenly available.

The three species of fishes mentioned above are certainly not candidates for anyone's list of dangerous fishes. They do emphasize, however, that when abnormal conditions exist and people happen to be present, otherwise harmless fish can cause trouble. The trapped Spanish mackerel, the ravenous bluefish, and the startled mullet do serve to establish the fact that no one can say with positive assurance just what any creature of the sea is always going to do. It cannot be denied that fishermen occasionally stretch the truth, but many are the times on the water when things happen that are not easily explained.

The other fishes that will be discussed in this chapter are different only because they have established a record of causing trouble for people by specialized means. It can be stated, almost without exception, that if not molested or unduly excited most fishes are content to go about their normal routine without causing trouble for humans who invade their domain. The most decided exception is the shark, and because it is so different, it will be discussed in a separate chapter.

Because of the possible serious consequences, swimmers, skin divers, and fishermen should exercise caution in handling or molesting any creature of the sea until he knows for sure it is safe to do so. It is also important for the human who values his safety not to place himself in the path of danger. Such a warning may seem redundant, but statistics prove that this is the reason most injuries are received from creatures of the sea.

Barracuda

The barracuda, especially the large ones such as the great barracuda, *Sphyraena barracuda,* is often referred to as the "tiger of the sea." It is an apt analogy in some respects and one that is readily accepted by anyone who has observed its method of attack on other fish. It will lurk motionlessly in some place of concealment until something it considers edible comes within range. It will then launch itself from a dead standstill, occasionally cutting its prey in half, only to return a moment later to pick up what is left and dart away so swiftly that it seems to vanish.

Witnessing such an attack from a pier or while out in a boat has a discouraging effect on many people who might have been planning to go for a swim. Many believe the barracuda is as dangerous as a shark. There is no question that people are occasionally injured, sometimes severely so, by this fish, and there are records that indicate that the attacks have been fatal from time to time. Unlike sharks, it is doubtful the barracuda would ever attack a human with the intentions of eating him. If it happens to cut off a hand or mangle a leg, it is almost certain that it would be an impromptu attack. In all probability it might see some portion of human anatomy and momentarily mistake it for a fish, but in that brief space of time the damage would be done.

In the western hemisphere the great barracuda is found from the North Carolina coast, south throughout the Gulf of

Barracuda.

Mexico, well distributed in the Caribbean, and down along the Brazilian coast. Another similar species is found from Hawaii across to the Red Sea. Off the coast of California the Pacific barracuda, *Sphyraena argentea,* is plentiful. It is rated as an excellent food and game fish and represents no threat to swimmers and skin divers. These are not nearly so large as those found in other parts of the world.

The great barracuda of the Atlantic will reach a length of six feet and weigh well over a hundred pounds. Like the moray, they will occasionally feed extensively on puffer fish which cause their flesh to become highly toxic. Since there is no test to prove whether or not the flesh is poisonous, it is unwise to risk eating them, especially those from tropical waters.

The Sieur de Rochefort published a book in 1665 titled *Natural History of the Antilles.* His observations of the barracuda found in the Caribbean waters leave little doubt that he considered it to be a highly dangerous fish. His views differ from those of researchers and observers who have followed, but the following passage is worthy of note.

Amonge the monsters greedy and desirous of human flesh, which are found on the coasts of the islands [West Indies] the Becune [barracuda] is one of the most formidable. It is a fish which has the figure of a pike, and which grows to six or eight feet in length and has a girth in proportion. When it perceives its prey, it launches itself in fury, like a bloodthirsty dog, at the men it has perceived in the water. Furthermore it is able to carry away a part of that which it has been able to catch, and its teeth have so much venom that the smallest bite becomes mortal if one does not have recourse at that very instant to some powerful remedy in order to abate and turn aside the force of the poison.

Again there is the mention of a fish with venomous teeth, and it is still believed by many in some areas. It is not true if the word "venom" is intended to be synonymous with true venom, as from the fang of a poisonous snake. The possibility of a tetanus-type infection is very real and precaution should be taken.

Nearly a century later, in 1742, another observer, Père Labat, made his comments on the barracuda.

As it is not obliged to turn on its side like the shark when it wishes to bite, it is infinitely more dangerous. Our savages, who attack and kill Requins [sharks] and Pantoufliers [hammerhead

Puffer.

sharks] with knives, do not dare to run that risk with Becunes [barracudas], because, moving with such extraordinary speed, they carry away an arm, a leg, or a head as if they had been cut off with a blow of a sabre. It has happened several times that horses and other animals crossing [the Gallion River] by swimming have had their legs cut off or half their bellies carried away.

The tooth structure of the barracuda is remarkable and this combined with its speed and powerful jaws make it a formidable living weapon. Even if Père Labat did fall into the trap of believing that sharks must turn on their sides to bite, he was right when he said that no one would go after a barracuda with a knife. Swimming sharks can and have been stabbed and even sliced with a knife, but I have yet to see a human swimmer fast and agile enough to even touch a barracuda.

The teeth are knifelike, in single rows in each side of the mouth, and the cutting teeth are sharply edged, both forward and backward. Aristotle knew the barracuda and gave it the name *sphyraena,* which is from the Greek word *sphyra,* meaning pickhammer. This was in reference to the canine teeth in the front of the top and lower jaws. These teeth are spikelike and their primary purpose is to halt a fast-swimming fish. There immediately follows an almost instant second bite which often severs the prey.

It is not difficult to distinguish the bite of a barracuda from that of a shark. The latter is likely to be ragged and torn, while the barracuda's teeth usually make a smoother cut. It is necessary to say *usually,* because if the fish should make a head-on attack on the body of a human the wound would likely be in the form of flesh torn by the canine teeth. Such an attack might likely occur when the barracuda had spotted the glint of a belt buckle or some other bright article of attire.

Those who have been slashed by barracuda have frequently remarked that they hardly realized they had been bitten until they saw the flow of blood. On July 14, 1960, a twenty-four-year-old skin diver, Bob Allen, was attacked by one about two hundred yards offshore near Pompano Beach,

Florida. Allen said the fish, which he immediately recognized to be a large barracuda, made a swift attack, striking him first on one of his legs, then turning quickly, it slashed his arm. Allen reported the bites were much like being cut with a razor. He was rushed to a hospital and thirty stitches were required to close the two wounds. This was a typical attack in still another aspect. The barracuda apparently realized after the second strike that it had made a mistake and swam away quickly with no effort made to pursue the attack.

Numerous accounts of these fish attacking humans have been verified, running the gamut from minor to severe to fatal. Serious researchers understandably want positive proof. Often, such proof is next to impossible to establish for several reasons. Unlike the shark that may circle and allow time for witnesses to see it, the barracuda's attack is swift. The victim himself is usually too preoccupied to make a careful observation. Further still, many people who might have actually witnessed the attack would be able only to say that it was a large fish.

When an attack by some sea creature results in death to the victim, it is often debatable just how dependable any witnesses may be. All too often some of the most relevant information is omitted, thus casting a shadow of doubt over other details. Occasionally something as important as the victim's name is not included in the report.

One glaring example of such an omission concerns a fatal attack that occurred off Key West, Florida, in 1952. There were witnesses, including those who attempted a rescue, who were believed to be reliable, but they failed to add two important facts. First, the man's name was not known and no one bothered to list the exact date. The victim was locally known to be a pilot for Pan American Airlines. There can be little doubt that a coroner's report was filed and there must have been some hospital record, but the name and date remain a mystery.

Several people saw the pilot begin thrashing about in the water. They noted that he was wearing a pair of fluorescent-hued swimming trunks. Several men hurried to a boat and went out to help, thinking perhaps that he was in trouble with a shark. When they arrived a large barracuda was seen close to the surface, apparently watching the man who was still alive, but bleeding badly. They said the fish gave no indication of further aggression, but neither did it seem inclined to leave. The pilot had been severely slashed in the region of the groin and died as he was being taken to the Boca Chica Naval Hospital. If it was the barracuda that was responsible for the attack, it can be guessed that it was attracted to the bright swimming trunks.

An earlier official record of a barracuda attack is considerably more complete in some details, but here the witnesses could only say the attack was made by a large fish. It was the afternoon of June 6, 1924, and the victim was twenty-three-year-old Anthony Sjalkiewicz who was a navy carpenter's mate. He and several companions were swimming near the Coco Solo Naval Base. The others had left the water and were on the beach waiting for Sjalkiewicz when he began to shout for help. Those watching caught sight of a large fish and by the time they had the carpenter's mate ashore their main concern was to rush him to the base hospital. His right leg was sliced open from the knee to the middle of the calf. As it happened, the noted marine biologist Charles M. Breder was at the hospital when the victim was admitted. He made a careful examination of the wound and concluded it had been made by a barracuda. Although he almost died from loss of blood, Sjalkiewicz survived. Nearness to medical aid and speedy assistance from his companions were responsible.

Boating a large barracuda is an open invitation for a serious bite. As with many fish, it will flounce about and snap savagely at anything within range. Many conservation-minded fishermen will release any fish they do not wish to make use of in one way or another. Considerably more caution than usual is recommended when a barracuda is to be returned to the water. At times, even those who should know better will become careless and I do not exclude myself from this group.

An incident when I failed to follow the rules occurred when my wife and I were fishing with Col. O. E. Henderson off the south tip of Anclote Key out from Tarpon Springs, Florida. I was using spinning tackle and a small yellow plug. On one of the casts I hooked a barracuda that was about three feet long. The fight was lengthy, and when I had it close to the boat I reached over, snagged it with a gaff, and lifted it out of the water.

For a moment the three of us examined the fish, remarked on the size of its teeth and especially its smell, which many barracuda possess. For some reason not all Atlantic barracuda have this smell. Those of the eastern Pacific have a nice clean fish odor and are not at all repulsive like some of their Atlantic relatives.

In a momentary lapse of common sense, I reached over with my left hand and was about to grasp the small lure to twist it free. Just as my hand was nearing the fish's mouth it twisted and slapped its jaws shut on my fingers. I was, of course, in no dire peril, but I was in an unpleasant predicament. If I had released my grip on the gaff handle, I would have had the entire weight of the fish hanging onto my left fingers.

In an effort to assist, my wife ripped a towel in half and used it to protect her own hands as she tried to pry the jaws apart. It only caused the fish to increase its struggle. Eventually, Col. Henderson slipped the blade of a sheath knife between the jaws at the hinge and twisted. The leverage forced the jaws open just enough for me to get my fingers free. They bled profusely, and after washing them I poured antiseptic over the punctures. Having recently had a tetanus shot, I saw no reason for further attention and luckily none was needed.

The barracuda is a master at an odd form of camouflage. At times they can, seemingly at will, become ghostlike with only their large eyes and the black splotches on their sides visible. When hanging motionlessly in the water in this condition they blend so perfectly with the bottom that they will be unseen unless one knows to look for the shadow they cast on the bottom.

Skin divers and wading anglers will occasionally experience a form of nervous tension when they turn to discover a large barracuda that appears to be stalking them. At times they will turn and vanish in a flash if one waves an arm or kicks at them. But, again, the tension mounts if they refuse to be frightened away and simply hold steady, as if spoiling for a fight.

It can be decidedly unnerving to be dogged by one or more that are large enough to cause serious injury if they should decide to attack. I have been in the water when one takes up station and seems to be studying every move I make. Many people who have found themselves in this situation will excitedly tell of being chased out of the water by a barracuda displaying such curiosity. To say *chased* is really a poor choice of words, since no human could move fast enough to exceed the speed of one of these fish if it decided to make an attack. More accurately, they were simply frightened out of the water.

Beyond the sheer carelessness of letting the gaffed barracuda bite me, I strongly suspect the closest I have come to serious injury was once while I was fishing from a small skiff

Wading bonefish angler.

Barracuda just below surface.

near the Ten Thousand Islands off the lower west coast of Florida. When I do not have an ice chest aboard I make a practice of eviscerating any fish I catch if it is intended for the table. I do not mean I do so immediately, but I try to do this within the first half hour after they are caught. To do so retards spoilage and the flesh retains a better flavor.

On this particular day I had boated two snook, each weighing about five pounds. I cleaned the first one, leaned over the gunwale and washed it in the water. A couple of minutes later I was washing the second snook, holding it by the tail and swishing it back and forth in the water. Suddenly, the fish was snatched from my grasp and I saw a barracuda that must have measured nearly four feet in length about three yards off to the starboard side.

It paused for a moment near the surface with my gutted snook in its jaws, then vanished into deep water. Had the fish been smaller, or if the barracuda had misjudged its attack by a matter of inches, my hand might have been included in his piscatorial pilfering. I still give boated fish a preliminary cleaning, but since that time I never wash one in the water beside the boat without a certain apprehension.

Sea Catfish

Almost everyone who has fished, even occasionally, in salt water has had the misfortune of hooking a sea catfish. They are scaleless, somewhat slimy nuisances, of only fair food value, and about as sporting to catch as an old tennis shoe. As if that were not enough to place it at the bottom of the list, sea catfish are dangerous and each year countless people are injured by its venomous spines.

There is one species of sea catfish popularly known as the gafftopsail, *Bagre marinus,* found in the Atlantic with close relatives in the Pacific, that approaches the requirements of a game fish, and the flesh is quite palatable. These, too, have venomous spines and because they are larger and more active, should be handled with as much or more caution.

The one most common in the Atlantic, Gulf of Mexico, and Caribbean, *Galeichthys felis,* probably causes the most trouble because it is so numerous. It is quite likely that thousands of people are injured each year. Most are minor wounds, but a percentage are serious and, despite the size of the fish, they should be handled with care.

The reason so many people are injured is that these catfish resemble several of the numerous species of freshwater catfish. The angler has likely had experience with the freshwa-

Gafftopsail catfish.

Common sea catfish.

ter variety and avoids the spines just as he would the fins of
any fish, but does not consider them serious.

Sea catfish have three venomous spines. One is located
near the anterior part of the dorsal fin and the others are in
each of the pectoral fins. When first caught these spines are
usually erect and the tips are exposed. The three fins can be
locked in this position whenever the fish elects to do so and
they may remain erect even after death. At times the fish will
be caught and thoughtlessly tossed up on the beach or on the
deck of a pier, where they lie as a potential threat to anyone
who may step on them.

It is doubtful that swimmers are ever injured by catfish unless they happen to step on a dead or disabled one that has
been caught and discarded in shallow water. The catfish
could not by any measure be considered aggressive and will
attempt to escape from any creature that exceeds them in
size. Thus, if they are in a normal state of health, it would be
nearly impossible to accidentally step on one.

They are fundamentally scavenger fish that find most of
their food on or near the bottom. The fact that they will eat
almost anything, coupled with their abundance, is the reason
so many are hooked. The basic danger comes in handling
them once they have been caught.

Anyone who has seen a freshwater catfish would have no difficulty in recognizing the saltwater variety. They grow to a length of approximately one and a half feet, but the average is about half this size. They are bluish black on the back, fading to a dull white underneath. There are four harmless barbels, one on each side of the mouth and a smaller pair attached to the bottom of the lower jaw.

The gafftopsail catfish, mentioned earlier, is somewhat larger with a much wider head and is easily distinguished by the long filaments extending from the dorsal and pectoral fins. It is a partial bottom feeder, but will frequently strike artificial lures as well as trolled bait.

The venomous spines of all sea catfish are slightly serrated on the sides and, except for the sharp points, are encased in an integumentary sheath. The glandular poison cells are in this thin membrane and when any of the three spines is driven into flesh the cells rupture, allowing the venom to be introduced into the victim's flesh.

If the wound is shallow the spine is usually withdrawn and the injury is slight. In more severe cases, such as might be encountered by stepping on the catfish, the spine may be driven in so deeply that it is broken off. In such an event the victim is not only envenomated with considerably more poison but there is the problem of removing the spine.

Almost invariably, due to the serrated edges along the sides, a surgical operation is necessary for safe removal. Attempting to grasp the spine with a pair of pliers and forcefully withdraw it is only to subject the victim to considerable pain and excessive tissue damage. Even a skilled surgeon, with all of the necessary equipment, does not find the removal of a deeply imbedded spine a simple task. It is certainly not one that should be attempted by a fellow fisherman in the cockpit of a boat or along the beach.

Over many years of saltwater fishing, I have caught and handled countless catfish. On infrequent occasions, when I have allowed myself to become careless, I have been pricked and scratched by these dangerous spines. At such times the resulting pain has ranged from barely noticeable to moderately annoying. Some years ago, however, while my wife and

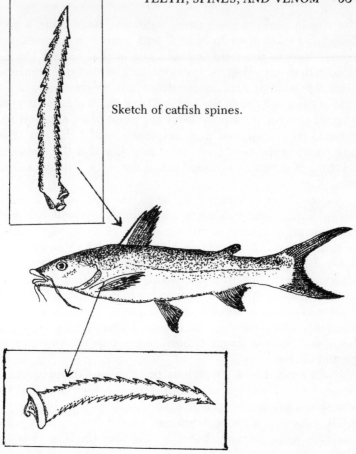

Sketch of catfish spines.

I were surf fishing along the northwest coast of Florida, I had the unwelcome experience of proving that a puncture wound from one of these spines can be decidedly unpleasant.

The episode began when my wife hooked and beached a large catfish that weighed about three pounds. Noticing that she was encountering difficulty in removing the hook with the aid of a piece of driftwood and a pair of pliers, I set my own tackle aside and walked over to relieve her of the task.

Grasping the fish by the caudal peduncle, I gripped the hook with the pliers and twisted it free. I should have tossed the catfish back out into deep water and been done with it. Instead, I continued to hold it and carelessly allowed it to come close to my right leg and just at that instant the fish flounced in an effort to break free. The weight, combined with the sudden movement, drove one of the pectoral fins into my leg just above the knee. There was a momentary stab of pain similar to running afoul the point of an exposed nail. Beyond that it seemed inconsequential and I did not attach any significance to it. I was glad to notice that the spine had not broken off and I assumed it had not made a deep penetration.

A moment or so later my attention was attracted to a surface disturbance a short distance away that suggested fish were feeding on a school of minnows. Picking up my tackle I began walking swiftly in that direction. I had gone only a short distance when I became increasingly conscious of an abnormal sensation that seemed to be spreading through my entire right leg. The first symptom was one of abnormal chill. This was quickly amplified by a pins-and-needles feeling, similar to that commonly experienced when an arm or leg has been constrained in an abnormal position for an extended period of time.

Right away I was suspicious that the catfish fin might be responsible. I paused to examine the wound and noted that the skin surrounding the puncture had become blanched. I tried to ignore it and concentrate on the direction in which the fish were moving, but the cold and tingling sensation continued to spread until it seemed to cover the entire right side of my body.

My next unpleasant discovery was that I was losing control of my fingers and the right leg was becoming paralyzed. Spotting a small tree a short distance back from the beach, I hobbled toward the limited circle of shade and sat down. As I tried to rest I became aware of a sharp acid taste in my mouth and again I examined the wound. The patch of pallid flesh had, in the space of about three minutes, changed to a circle of red and the area was sensitive to touch. Breathing was becoming difficult, and as I lay down on my back I realized I was so dizzy that the entire world seemed to be cartwheeling before my eyes.

As the minutes passed a growing nausea engulfed me and I began to vomit. I attempted to call to my wife, but my vocal cords would not function. For the next quarter hour or so my body was as hot as it might have been if I had been severely sunburned. My pulse had become rapid and was pounding so hard I could feel it throbbing in my neck and the sides of my head.

Quite suddenly I realized I was perspiring profusely and shortly after this development I began to notice I was feeling more normal. I had not recorded the time, but when I was again able to move about I walked back to where my wife was fishing. She had seen me go lie down in the shade and had thought I had simply decided to take a short nap. We estimated that I had been there for something over half an hour. The only aftereffects were the metallic taste in my mouth and a mild soreness around the wound, both of which lasted for about two days.

Because of the varying degree of severity in connection with the poisonous spines of the sea catfish, it is difficult to state precisely how much attention should be given to such a wound. Minor injury can usually be satisfactorily handled by washing thoroughly with salt water. The use of antiseptic should be used to reduce the danger of secondary infection. In the case of deeper penetration, especially when the above mentioned symptoms become severe, the victim should seek medical aid.

It behooves anyone fishing in salt water to learn to handle a catfish once it has been hooked and landed. Many experienced anglers have learned the proper way to grasp one so that the spines do not present a threat. A still safer method is to use a pair of fish grippers that will protect the hands while the hook is being removed.

Proper disposal of a catfish, once it has been caught, cannot be overemphasized. No one with any regard for others will leave it where it can be stepped on. Since it ranks low as food—excepting the gafftopsail cat—it is impractical to keep.

It can be just as dangerous in the ice chest as when freshly caught. In open water, away from swimming beaches, it may be tossed back in and forgotten. At first this may seem a wasteful procedure, but it should be remembered that no form of flesh goes to waste in salt water. If the catfish is dead there will always be scavengers waiting to feed on it. Often these forms of life will, in turn, become a source of food for humans or other more valuable forms of fish life.

Jewfish

Any fish objects to being taken from the water. All have some means of defending themselves, whether it be teeth, spines, sharp gill covers, venom, or a slimy coating. Most depend first on their speed and agility to enable them to escape and resort to their defense weapons only when they are restrained. In the overall picture, only a very small percentage can cause injury beyond a minor flesh wound.

Once in a while certain fish that are considered virtually harmless will suddenly react in a decidedly atypical manner. One good example is the huge jewfish, *Epinephelus itajara*, that is known to attain a weight of over seven hundred pounds. Visitors to aquariums will look with awe at one of these giant groupers and, if they are newcomers to the world of fish, will be surprised to learn that such a ponderous creature is rated as harmless.

Ninety-nine percent of the time the jewfish presents a problem in catching simply because many of them are so large that hauling them aboard a boat requires considerable work. In years of fishing, skin diving, and spearfishing I have caught many of them and never observed an aggressive act. The thought that one would swallow a man seemed as preposterous as being bitten by a guppy.

Professional divers, especially those who work around the bottom of offshore oil rigs, generally encounter enough genuine problems in their line of work. So many, in fact, that they do not feel called upon to concoct wild tales just for the fun of it. A personal friend of mine, Nick Zinkowski, is a mas-

Jewfish.

ter diver and one of the best in the business. His encounter
with a jewfish was as much of a surprise to him as it was to
those who heard of his unusual experience. It was fortunate
for Nick that he had a witness, because not only could his
diving companion corroborate his story but probably saved
his life.

The two men were working out of a diving bell with a
hatch on the bottom through which they could enter and exit.
They were down near the base of an oil platform when the
strange performance began. They first became puzzled when
a jewfish of giant proportions began sticking the front part of
its head up through the open hatch. After doing this several
times the big fish seemed to have satisfied its curiosity and
apparently departed. A few minutes later Nick left the bell
and began working around the base of the tower. He had
hardly had time to get started when he noticed the inquisitive jewfish return to the lighted area and begin examining
him with what Nick considered too much interest. Unable to
frighten the fish away, he decided to delay his underwater
work temporarily and return to the bell. Just as he was climbing inside the jewfish grabbed him by both legs.

Nick's companion immediately sensed the seriousness of the problem and grabbed him by the shoulders. As he pulled one way the fish was pulling the other, almost as if he might have been inhaling Nick—and Nick is not a small man. The two divers won the struggle, but the huge grouper did manage to pull off a boot. Eventually Nick decided to venture out again and this time the fish was gone, but so was the boot. The fish may have swallowed it during the struggle or carried it away and dropped it.

Several months later two other divers were working in the same area from a similar bell and under almost the same conditions. Again the diver saw a large jewfish approaching and he beat a hasty retreat toward the bell. It was almost a repeat performance, except this time the fish got all of the man inside his cavernous mouth. The other diver inside the bell began pulling on the lifeline and once more the fish decided to relinquish its prize. In a matter of seconds the diver was able to scramble into the safety of the bell—an unharmed but frightened "Jonah."

Whether either of the two men would actually have been ingested, or whether the fish would have spit them out of their own free will is open to speculation. In neither case was the fish molested and their action must be classed as unprovoked attacks. As the interest in skin diving and spearfishing increases, so do the number of accounts that suggest large jewfish may not be as docile as has long been believed.

Their range is the Gulf of Mexico and tropical waters in the Caribbean and western Atlantic. The depth at which they are found is quite varied. Reefs, rock piles, sunken wrecks, and other underwater obstructions are natural haunts. Deep or shallow, the only requirement is that the place attracts large numbers of fish for the jewfish to feed upon without too much of a chase.

Billfish

Billfish, which include sailfish, marlin, and swordfish, are at the top of the list where spectacular big game fishing is concerned. The blue marlin, *Makaira ampla,* and the

(Top to bottom) Blue marlin, white marlin, swordfish, sailfish.

swordfish, *Xiphias gladius,* far exceed the sailfish, *Istiophorus americanus,* in size. All, however, possess a long spear of hard bone which is an extension of the upper jaw.

Tales of swordfish ramming ships and driving their spears through heavy hull planking reach far back into the history of seafaring. Some nautical museums have sections cut from the hulls of ships, with the imbedded spear, to bear mute testimony to the power of both the marlin and swordfish. Both are occasionally referred to as swordfish incorrectly.

Although these fish could easily kill a human with their weapons, they have never been known to do so deliberately. Whenever people are injured in connection with these fish it involves the frantic attempt of the fish to escape from a hook, especially when one is being drawn close to the boat. It is thought the reason they attack ships and sometimes large whales is because they are startled and ram their spears from fright, rather than a desire to kill. There would be no natural reason for such attacks, since their diet consists of school fish, such as jacks and mackerel, and fish that can be swallowed whole.

When people are occasionally injured it is generally a case where they have had just enough experience to feel they can handle billfish, but not enough to expect the unexpected. Two fishing companions, Al Jennings and Ashley Lofler, were with me when we had a serious encounter with a white marlin, *Makaira albida,* while we were trolling from a forty-one-foot cabin boat in the Gulf out from the little town of Destin, Florida.

The three of us were experienced bluewater fishermen and were well aware of the potential danger of bringing a large billfish aboard without exercising proper precautions. We had the big fish securely hooked and were making preparations to boat it. This is always a critical moment in this type of fishing and one that should never be approached carelessly. What made our encounter somewhat different was that even before any of us touched the fish, it surged up in a jump that carried it over the gunwale. Lofler and I succeeded in dodging safely, but Jennings wound up in the hos-

Marlin, jumping.

Blue marlin being boated.

pital emergency ward and barely missed being killed in the cockpit of the boat.

Our mistake had come in our failure to attach significant importance to the fact that the marlin had not put up a typical fight. In later analysis we concluded that it did not become seriously perturbed until it was close to the boat. It might normally have been expected to turn and make a scorching run, but this one simply put all of its energy into that final jump. The spear struck Jennings on the left side of his chest and severely gashed his left arm just below the shoulder. Had the impact been just a bit more to the right, the spear would have plunged into his heart.

Similar injuries have occurred when this type of fish is being hauled over the gunwale. It is highly doubtful they attach any importance to a human. They are making a bid for freedom and if a person happens to be in the way he is going to have to pay for his carelessness. Marlin are rambunctious and powerful, scatter-brained, and potentially as dangerous as a stick of dynamite with a lighted fuse, which is probably what makes them such a marvelous game fish. Van Campen Heilner, who pioneered in the sport of fishing for them nearly half a century ago, called them "the rhinoceros of the sea."

Swordfish held by Capt. Bill Gray.

John Josselyn wrote a book titled *Account of Two Voyages to New England,* which was published in 1674. His description of a swordfish attacking a ship is as follows:

> The twentieth day in the afternoon we saw a great fish called Vehuella or Sword-fish, having a long strong and sharp finn like a sword-blade on the top of his head, with which he pierced our ship and broke it off striving to get loose.

The Greek writer Oppian, who penned at least five books on fish and fishing in the second century, knew the swordfish and in one of his didactic poems he quite aptly summed up the general feeling that has persisted down through the ages when he wrote:

> Nature her Bounty to his mouth confin'd
> Gave him a sword, but left unarmed his mind.

Needlefish

Almost everyone who spends any time on or in salt water is familiar with one or more of the numerous species of needlefish. Most are small and harmless to man, with their chief value being their use as bait for larger fish. They are of the family Belonidae and are widely distributed around the world. As their name implies, they are slim and easily distinguished by their enlongated jaws, well studded with small sharp teeth. In most species the bottom jaw is slightly longer than the upper and they feed extensively on smaller surface swimming fish.

The largest member of the needlefish family is popularly known as the houndfish. A large one may reach a length of about five feet and weigh as much as fifteen pounds. These and other large species will readily strike lures designed to work on or near the surface. For a relatively small fish, they put on a spectacular fight as they leap and tailwalk across the water. If carelessly handled after being caught they can inflict a painful bite, but this is not their primary danger.

Like all needlefish, they spend the majority of their time close to the surface and, especially at night, they are easily startled. The approach of a boat will send them leaping across the surface and often, if there is a bright light showing, they will tend to jump toward it. As previously mentioned, other fish, such as mullet, will react in a similar manner, but where large needlefish, such as the houndfish, are concerned such action can be considerably more dangerous. They move at a high rate of speed and there have been numerous reports of serious injury when a boat occupant is the accidental target of one of these living spears.

Since it is impractical to build a suitable shield around an open boat, there is little that can be done to avoid the possibility of being injured by these fish. They are mentioned only to demonstrate how people can occasionally be injured by otherwise harmless fish. In daylight hours they will almost invariably dart away from an approaching boat.

Surgeonfish

Fish do not have to be large or ugly to be dangerous, and at times the defensive weapons can be unusual in their location. The surgeonfish, of the family Acanthuridae, is a classic example of one that can inflict a painful injury in an unexpected manner.

Most people who have been bitten, finned, and had their hands cut by sharp gill covers, will look toward the tail area as being safe. Also, the caudal peduncle on the average fish is the smallest part of the body and affords a natural "handle" to grasp fish that have been caught.

This is exactly the *wrong* place to lay hold of a surgeonfish, and anyone who tries it is almost certain to withdraw a hand bleeding from deep wounds. The reason is a unique pair of weapons that resemble the blades of a pocketknife. In certain species these razor-sharp spines are permanently erected, but in many of the others they are cleverly concealed until needed.

When surgeonfish with the moveable spines are calmly nudging the side of a reef feeding on algal growth, which constitutes the major part of their diet, the dangerous blades are hidden from view. When danger threatens they spring into position almost as swiftly as the opening of a switch-blade knife.

The location of these sharp weapons are on each side of the caudal peduncle with the hinge near the base of the tail. When the blades are closed they fit into open-sided sheaths or grooves in the flesh. The pointed ends are directed forward, and when erect they extend laterally.

Skin divers exploring coral reefs and rock piles have discovered, much to their distress, that it is not always necessary to actually grasp a surgeonfish to be injured. If startled by an outstretched hand, the blades spring open and the fish lashes its tail from side to side. If it makes contact with flesh there is sure to be blood in the water.

Because of their vegetarian diet, hook and line fishermen are not likely to haul one aboard. Even this cannot be ruled out entirely because occasionally they are snagged as the hook is being drawn to the surface.

The most common of these fish in Atlantic waters is the blue tang, *Acanthurus coeruleus,* and is known to range as far north as New York, becoming increasingly more numerous to the south. They are common in Bermuda and well distributed throughout the Caribbean.

The shape of many species is similar to the common freshwater sunfish with vertically compressed bodies. The dorsal and anal fins are extensive along the top and bottom sides of the fish. The tails differ from slightly lunate to those with exaggerated streamers on both upper and lower tips. These streamers are particularly noticeable in the Indo-Pacific genera and especially *Naso lituratus* which is found throughout Polynesian waters, across to the east coast of Africa. *Naso* is also a surgeonfish that has fixed spines on the caudal peduncle and instead of one on each side, there are two.

This form of posterior armament is particularly useful to these fish because their heads are often tucked into cracks

Surgeonfish, blue tang.

and crevices as they search for food. In this position, they would be easy targets for other reef-dwelling fish were it not for their unusual form of protection.

Scorpionfish

Rated as the most venomous of all fishes in the sea is the group commonly known as scorpionfish (*Scorpaena*), which include zebrafish, (*Pterois*) and stonefish (*Synanceja*). All are of the family Scorpaenidae and are found worldwide in tropical, subtropical, and some temperate waters. The zebrafish, *Pterois antennata*, is also known as the turkeyfish, lionfish, and tigerfish. It is decidedly the most colorful of all, with a ground color of red, streaked with jet black marks and irregular snow white patches. The various fins are abnormally large and ornate, reminding one of a strutting turkey or peacock. In contrast is the deadly stonefish, *Synanceja verrucosa*, which

Scorpionfish.

is about as drab and ugly as any fish that can be found. It is broad across the head with rounded, almost winglike, pectoral fins and it tapers abruptly to a stubby tail. Most measure less than a foot in length and weigh about two pounds. It is as if nature, or some inept helper, attempted to fashion a fish and became disgusted with the progress, leaving the lumpy experiment unfinished.

What the stonefish lacks in aesthetic beauty, however, is more than compensated for in danger. This comes in the form of short venomous spines on the pelvic and anal fins and a dozen or more that extend along the back. So potent is its poison that there have been numerous reliable reports that a stab of only one of these spines caused almost instant death.

Even if the injury happens not to be fatal it can cause extensive suffering for the unlucky victim.

To illustrate the agonizing effects of stonefish venom, an incident experienced by Dr. J. L. B. Smith is worth relating. He is the same ichthyologist who, in the company of Miss M. Courtenay-Latimer, astounded the world with the discovery and identification of the coelacanth. The discovery of the coelacanth has no bearing on Dr. Smith's encounter with the stonefish, except to prove that even highly knowledgeable marine biologists are occasionally severely wounded in a moment of carelessness by a fish they know to be dangerous. It is also valuable from a scientific standpoint, since the report was written by a man who would not be disposed to exaggerate the extent of danger involving a fish.

The incident occurred while Dr. Smith was collecting fish in the shallows off Portuguese East Africa. It was part of a

Stonefish.

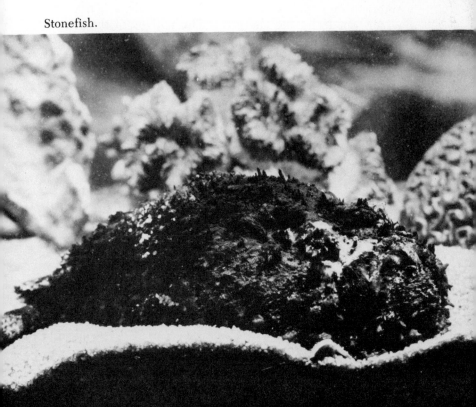

research program for a book he was writing about fish of African waters. One might be led to believe that no one, knowing the potential danger, would deliberately put his hand near such a fish. It is, however, much the same as an experienced herpetologist who seemingly handles the deadliest of reptiles in a casual manner. As with snakes, it is possible, and often necessary where fish are concerned, to forego the use of nets and snares. To do so may cost one his life, but it is done from time to time. For instance, it is possible to safely lift a stonefish from the water simply by sliding the hand beneath the fish's body and gripping it firmly by closing the fingers and thumb on the sides to prevent its escape. It is a feat that one seldom has a chance to practice up on if one makes a mistake.

There is always the chance that the fish may react in an unexpected manner. Each spine on the stonefish has an anterior groove connected to a venom sac and each is covered by an integumental sheath. The slightest pressure breaks this membrane and the venom instantly flows upward into the puncture made by the sharp tip. The natives of the region where Dr. Smith was collecting call the stonefish the "sherova" and many do not hesitate to catch them barehanded. Here is Dr. Smith's account:

At tide pools we usually worked by applying poison, leaving the natives to collect the fishes as we worked from one pool to the next. On August 19, 1950, at about 3 P.M., a boy called out "sherova," and was told to keep it. About half an hour later, having a tube of rarer form in my hand and wishing to go and inspect the catches in canoes from the outer reef, I called the nearest boy and, reaching up to the tray on his head, put the tube in it, telling him to guard it from the sun. In doing this I felt a sharp stab in my thumb, and hastily withdrew thinking it had been due to a needle in the rag, and I felt it touch the bone. As I looked at two bleeding punctures, an intense stab of pain shot up my arm to my neck. This was 6 to 10 seconds after the stab. With foreboding I made the boy bend, lifted the cloth, and there was a stonefish, contrary to orders, in the tray. Moreover it was still alive, with 13 dorsal spines erect, the second and third free from the membrane, the third for about one-fourth of an inch. Hastily binding string tightly around the thumb, I cut across the punctures and sucked vigorously, telling an agile servant to run for my wife who was around the point. I set off for the lighthouse, sucking vigorously all the time, but before reaching the beach, only five minutes away, the pain was spreading through the hand, mainly across the knuckles, and was of an intensity never before experienced. Of the half-mile through the forest to the lighthouse, a fairly steep incline, there remains little recollection save a grim battle to remain conscious and of an insane desire to ease the mounting agony by rolling on the ground. At the lighthouse the keeper came to help me. The hand was numb and swelling fast. We managed to sterilize a syringe, but while trying to withdraw some Nupercain from the bottle, that fell and broke on the concrete floor. As I stood stupidly, my wife burst in and soon injected Novocain. For a short time this had some effect, but the pain had by now become a searing agony, mostly across the back of the hand, with spasms reaching the neck, head, and shoulder. The perspiration was such that my wife on arrival thought someone had splashed me with water, for it dripped to the floor. According to her account during the next two hours, of which I have little recollection, I was close to collapsing several times, but managed to keep on my feet. . . . At about two and one-half hours after the stab my wife injected $1/3$ grain morphine sulphate subcutaneously. After about twenty minutes I felt drowsy but the drug had no apparent effect on the pain. At about three and one-half hours after the stab, the pain was undiminished and the perspiration still profuse. My wife decided to try immersion in hot water. The effect was dramatic. The agony diminished rapidly to bearable proportions, and I returned to normal consciousness and an unquenchable thirst. We continued this immersion in hot water and I drank innumerable cups of tea for the next four hours, by which time the intense agony no longer recurred on removal from the hot water. In the morning the thumb was greatly enlarged, had turned black all around the area of the stabs, and was without sensation. The hand was greatly swollen, also the lower forearm, and was intensely painful to the touch. Twenty-four hours after the stab, large yellow blisters started to form and spread rapidly over the thumb, becoming exceedingly painful, and when punctured released a serous fluid, which dripped steadily thereafter for six days. The swelling gradually increased, reaching a maximum after three days, extending somewhat above the elbow. In this time joints and weak spots, such as old wounds, ached intensely all over the body. On the sixth day inflammation and pain in the thumb increased alarmingly and pus appeared. The injection of 1,000,000 units of penicillin in five doses over sixteen hours had a rapid and marked beneficial effect on the local condition, with retraction of the inflamed and blistered area . . .

On the ninth day some degree of sensation returned to the thumb. The blisters were subsiding and the swelling was no longer beyond the elbow. The hand was still swollen and painful. After fourteen days the hand and thumb only were still swollen, and painful and unusable. After thirty days the black portion commenced to fall away leaving pink scars. The site of the cut opened to a discharging cavity and did not heal finally until fifty days after the stab. After eighty days, the hand was still weak and the thumb barely moveable at the joints, being still slightly swollen and painful when moved. The toxin had a marked adverse effect on general health and condition.

Having been stabbed by an eagleray, *Myliobatis cervus* Smith, and by a barbel, *Tachysurus feliceps* Valenciennes, it is possible to say that *Synanceja* is in a class by itself. The fish which caused all this was 120 mm long and weighed 84 grams.

Since there is no specific antidote for stonefish venom, it can only be assumed that Dr. Smith survived probably because he did not receive a lethal amount of venom. Also, there can be no doubt that the capable medical assistance rendered by his wife was of immense value.

Members of Scorpaenidae are found from the shallows to a depth of well over a hundred feet. While the degree of virulence varies from one species to another, all are capable of inflicting serious injury. Despite the venom in their spines, some are valued as food fish and considered a worthwhile catch.

Eating these fish is not nearly as risky as it may seem since, like the flesh of rattlesnakes and other venomous serpents, the poison has no effect on the creature's flesh. It is important to reemphasize that there is a distinct difference between the safety of eating venomous fish and those with potentially toxic flesh. Logic, of course, dictates caution in handling and cleaning any fish with venomous spines.

Considering the extensive range of Scorpaenidae the logical question is, how likely is the possibility of a surf bather being injured? The chances are remote in recognized swimming waters where the bottom consists of sand or fine shell. Trouble is far more often encountered by venturesome individuals who elect to swim and wade in areas with rocks, coral formations, and other obstructions that afford suitable hiding places for fish that are inclined to lie in concealment while waiting for food to come their way.

Skin divers, wading anglers, and specimen collectors are more likely candidates for an unpleasant encounter. The skin diver soon learns to look carefully before touching bottom, the wading fisherman is repeatedly advised to move along by sliding his feet and those who wish to capture specimens for study or display should be sufficiently knowledgeable of their quarry.

Weeverfish

There are several species of weeverfish, all of the family Trachinidae. The two most well-known species are the greater weever, *Trachinus draco*, and the lesser weever, *Trachinus vipera*. Both are found over an extensive range from the North Sea, south along the British Isles, and throughout the Mediterranean and Black seas. Both of these weeverfish are similar in appearance, having a long body with eyes set near the top of the head and a second dorsal fin that begins just behind the venomous dorsal spines and extends almost to the tail. The anal fin is also quite long and extends along most of the underside of these fish.

The two primary differences are in the color and size, with the adult greater weever being nearly twice the size of the lesser. They are relatively small fish, seldom exceeding twenty and ten inches, respectively. The color of the greater is yellow with dark bands, while the smaller species is dull gray on the back, becoming noticeably paler on the underside. Another minor difference in general appearance is that the lesser weever's head is more upturned and closed jaws are only slightly forward of a vertical position.

The name weever is probably derived from the Anglo-Saxon word *wivre,* meaning viper. Such a comparison is appropriate, because the weeverfish actually strikes at its victims, but with its venomous fin spines instead of fangs. The greater is not of particular concern to anyone except fishermen who occasionally catch them and especially trawler fishermen who may be injured while removing fish from nets. It is a fish that swims in fairly deep waters, but is just as dangerous when brought aboard as when it is swimming free.

The lesser weever presents a more serious threat to a much larger number of people because it is frequently found in very shallow water. When resting and watching for food to come near it has a habit of covering most of its body with sand or mud, with only part of the head exposed. This trait makes them a double threat, since they may maintain this position and be stepped upon, or they may consider the approach of a wading human to represent some form of danger. At such times they may dart out of hiding, striking with the venomous opercular spines located on the rear of the gill covers.

The venom of the weeverfish is a combination of both neurotoxin and hemotoxin, reacting on both the nervous system and the blood. The dorsal spines number five to seven and, in outward appearance, are much the same as those on the majority of other fish. The dangerous spines are covered in a thin membranous sheath and pressure exerted upon the needle-sharp tips causes this sheath to be ruptured and the poison flows upward from the venom sacs located at the base of each spine.

It can be considered that the dangerous dorsal spines are specifically defensive weapons. The opercular spines on the gill covers seem to be designed to inflict serious injury and serve more as weapons of offense. There is little reason to suspect that any of the spines are used to subdue prey because the weevers are swift fish and feed on little fish they can easily capture without the aid of venom.

The apparent irritability of the weeverfish is somewhat of an exception where venomous fish are concerned. Most will attempt to avoid detection or seek a route of escape, depending on their venom to stop a deliberate attack. This cannot be said of the weevers, since they have been observed to take the offensive against larger creatures they could not make use of as food and were not causing them any trouble.

When these fish become excited the dorsal fins are immediately set in the erect position and the gill covers are expanded. Some who have been attacked have reported they saw the weever dart toward them and, even though an attempt was made, were unable to escape the decidedly accurate attack. Why they react in this manner is a mystery, unless they feel they have staked out their feeding ground and want to protect it from interlopers.

The effect of the venom instantly manifests itself in the form of a sharp pain that has been described as far exceeding that of a hornet sting. Instead of subsiding, the suffering increases with the passing minutes, generally reaching a peak in about half an hour. The area surrounding the puncture first becomes ashen in color, remains blanched for a few minutes, then becomes red and swollen.

Some human victims will be able to bear the pain without losing consciousness and may make an unassisted recovery in a matter of hours. Others, perhaps due to the amount of venom received or different body chemistry, will lapse into a stupor, be unable to speak, and perhaps go into convulsions.

In no case should the victim shun medical aid. This is important because of the possibility of so-called after shock that can dangerously reduce the rate of heartbeat and also severely impair the ability to breathe. A second reason is that there is a chance of secondary infection such as gangrene and other similar distress. Usually, however, the visit to a hospital will be sought because of the intense pain that continues to increase in the period following the injury.

There is no specific antivenin; thus medical assistance must rely on treating the important symptoms as they develop. In this respect, the venom of the weeverfish is much like that of other poisonous varieties.

The lesser weeverfish proves another exception to the rule in that they occasionally invade popular swimming areas. Fortunately, however, they are not numerous and do not constitute a serious threat. Because of the weever's aggressive attitude, the standard precaution of wading slowly and sliding the feet does not always cause the fish to flee. It may, instead, actually provoke it.

Toadfish

Members of the toadfish family, Batrachoididae, represent still another group, like the stonefish, that would seldom, if ever, be in the running if a piscatorial beauty contest were held. They can inflict very painful wounds, but fatalities are rare to the point of being almost nonexistent. However, their distribution is extensive and they should be avoided. Handling them in any way except with metal grippers is to invite trouble.

Toadfish are relatively small fish, with ones measuring a foot in length considered large. They vary in shape from one species to another. Some have broad heads and chunky bodies, while others are quite slender. All have large tooth-studded mouths with abnormally strong jaws that can inflict a painful, although not venomous, bite. The spines of the first dorsal fin are hollow with an opening at the side of the sharp tip. Two additional venomous spines are located on the gill covers, one on each side.

All of the spines resemble stubby hypodermic needles and the instant they penetrate flesh the venom is injected from individual sacs at the base. They are not aggressive, but are quick to bite if molested. If restrained they will flounce about, often bringing the opercular spine into play.

Their favorite habitats in most temperate, subtropical, and tropical waters are in and around rock piles, reefs, and places on the bottom where the vegetation offers concealment. They are seldom found in conventional swimming areas, but people wading across muddy and cluttered stretches of bottom should be on the lookout for them. Rubber-soled shoes offer suitable protection if one is stepped on, but the spines can easily penetrate the canvas sides.

Toadfish.

Those most frequently injured are fishermen who attempt to remove them from a line and skin divers who unwittingly touch them. The latter is not necessarily a careless act on the part of the diver, since some species of toadfish are skilled in camouflaging themselves. It is entirely possible to reach out and grasp what appears to be a rock, only to have it suddenly become a slick muscular body. In such case he may be painfully bitten or hit by a spine, or injured in both ways.

Their places of concealment are almost limitless and include an overhanging rock, clump of seaweed, sections of broken pipe, rusty tin cans, and even a glass jar if it is large enough for the toadfish to back into it. They lie almost motionless in such shelters waiting for some form of food to drift or swim close enough to be easily caught.

When one of the spines punctures the flesh the initial pain is severe. This soon subsides to a dull ache and the area around the wound becomes swollen. This is likely to persist for several hours, gradually becoming less noticeable. A bite from a moderately large toadfish usually tears a ragged gash on a person's fingers or toes. Because of the sluggish nature of these fish the teeth are almost certain to be more contaminated than those of more active types.

First-aid treatment for a bite should include a thorough washing and liberal application of antiseptic. There is no immediate treatment for a spine puncture, but neither the bite nor the poison should be dismissed simply because it has stopped hurting. A shot to prevent tetanus infection is important.

Ratfish

The ratfish, of which there are over two dozen species found around the world, is classed in a group known as Chimaeridae. They do not represent a serious threat anywhere in their extensive range, but they do have a long venomous spine in the anterior portion of the first dorsal fin. This spine is similar to the barbed type found on sea catfish and some members of the ray family. It is slightly recurved with barbs only on the posterior edge.

Ratfish are an oddity for a number of reasons. One of the most unusual features of the chimaeroids is that they have a cartilaginous skeleton instead of the bony frame of true fish. Because of this and other body features they were once incorrectly classed with sharks and rays. The dental formation is remarkably different in that the two front teeth in the upper jaw resemble those of a rodent, but are flattened and more chisel-shaped. If carelessly handled they can use these teeth to deliver a deep and painful bite.

Some ratfish are found in cold and very deep water as far

north as Alaska in the Pacific and Iceland in the Atlantic. Others frequent tropical waters and some are not uncommon off South Africa. Most species are grotesque with a large head and a body that tapers to a long slender tail. In a few species the tails resemble those of certain sharks. Many have eyes abnormally large for the size of the body. The length, depending on the species, may vary from less than a foot to over three feet. They have no scales, but unlike most sharks, the skin is smooth. They are not aggressive and are decidedly poor swimmers, making their way along with a curious twisting motion of the body.

The early Greeks, who examined and named so many forms of sea life, knew at least one species of the Chimaeridae. It is described in the *Iliad* as a female monster with a lion's head, a goat's middle, and the tail of a dragon. Despite their remarkable work in classifying sea animals, some of those scholars were not lacking in imagination and since fire breathing was almost a trademark of any self-respecting dragon, they apparently could not resist claiming this accomplishment for the misshapen fish.

There can be little or no argument that one of the most outlandishly constructed members of the chimaeroids is *Harriotta raleighana*. It grows to a length of four feet and is decidedly fusiform in shape with a long snout that tapers to a point, as does the long ratlike tail. The large eyes are above a comparatively small mouth. It is potbellied, and the dangerous spine of the first dorsal is located on the back above a pair of enlarged pectoral fins. At a point where the anal fin might be on an average fish there is an appendage that resembles the blade of a paddle which probably serves as a rudder, since the pointed tail would be of little value for changing directions.

Most ratfish are misshapen and ungainly, but it is interesting to note that they have the distinction of being among the most ancient fishlike creatures to inhabit the seas. They mate like sharks, with the male having a pair of claspers that are used to introduce the sperm into the female.

Stargazers

Stargazers are members of the family Uranoscopidae and possess a venomous spine on each shoulder just above the pectoral fins. They are doubly interesting as stinging fish in that they add an extra dimension in the form of an unpleasant electric shock. The potency of the venom varies widely from one species to another, ranging from simply a painful sting in some to occasional fatal envenomation inflicted by others.

The electric shock, while startling and mildly painful, is not dangerous to man. It is produced by a pair of organs located on the top of the head and can be compared to the negative and positive poles of the common wet-cell battery used in automobiles and other machinery. This miniature storage battery serves the stargazer in two ways. Primarily, it is a defense mechanism that quickly discourages any potential predator and can be used to stun small forms of sea life, thus enabling the stargazer to capture a percentage of its food without effort.

They are somewhat chunky fish, with some less than a foot in length, while others are half again as long. The body formation is not unusual, but the head structure is quite different from that of conventional fish. The eyes are positioned squarely on the top of the head so that the vision is directed upward, the feature which doubtlessly prompted the name. The jaws are similar to the weeverfish in that when closed they are almost vertical.

Both the eyes and jaws are ideally adapted to the stargazer's habit of lying partially buried in the sand or mud. With the eyes exposed and the jaws agape, the fish is immediately ready to capture any small creature that comes within range.

Different species of stargazers are to be found over a wide range that includes the eastern side of North and South America, the Mediterranean, and parts of the Pacific. The stout spines on the shoulders are grooved and encased in a thin sheath. When one of these enters the flesh the mem-

Stargazer.

brane is ruptured and the venom at the base flows upward along these grooves.

As with other creatures capable of producing an electric shock, the first contact is the strongest, becoming progressively weaker as its "battery" runs down. Stargazers caught in nets have generally exhausted their supply of current by the time they are hauled aboard. Experiments have proved, however, that if they are placed in tanks simulating their natural environment, the electric organs will go through a recharging cycle and the original voltage will return.

Stargazers are not aggressive and seldom frequent areas where people are swimming. Like many other fish, they will retreat if given sufficient warning. Their electric shock can be dismissed, but if one of the spines enters the flesh the pain will urge the victim to seek medical aid. Since it cannot be determined how much venom has been introduced and because fatalities have occurred, no such injury should be left untreated.

5

Sea Snakes

As with most dangerous sea creatures, considerable misinformation exists where venomous sea snakes are concerned. The facts are that sea snakes are unknown in the Atlantic and Caribbean, but they are present in the Pacific from the west coast of Central America all the way across to the east side of Africa. In some areas they are plentiful and some are decidedly dangerous. So dangerous, in fact, that the fatality rate has been pegged at 25 percent, meaning that one out of every four people who are bitten die as a result.

The distribution is one of the true oddities of nature. Throughout the tropical, subtropical, and temperate zones of the world both terrestrial and water snakes of numerous types are common. In the overall picture the vast majority are harmless serpents, some are mildly venomous, and still others are deadly. No one has ever been able to satisfactorily explain why the Atlantic and Caribbean are free of sea snakes.

It seems that since general conditions such as water temperature, topography, and suitable food are available in both bodies of water that the snakes would thrive equally as well, at least in the Caribbean, as they do on the Pacific side of

Central America. It is just another mystery of the sea that defies explanation.

Sea snakes are of the family Hydrophidae and include some fifty species. They have an extensive range that is bounded on the north by Japan, throughout the South Pacific, across the Indian Ocean, to the east coast of Africa. Only one species is known to live exclusively in fresh water. This is *Hydrophis semperi* found in Lake Taal on the Philippine island of Luzon.

As if to add to the confusion concerning distribution is that one important species that is found in parts of the above range has found its way across the vast open reaches of the Pacific. This is the yellow-bellied sea snake, *Pelamis platurus,* and is plentiful from the Gulf of California south to Peru. At times thousands of these may be seen in the Gulf of Panama.

Aware of this snake's apparent disregard for extensive travel, many herpetologists and marine biologists were confident that with the opening of the Panama Canal it would make the crossing and become established in the Caribbean. The first ship made that crossing on August 15, 1914, but to this date the threat has yet to materialize.

Even those who doubted that the snake would deliberately make the crossing admitted that it was not only possible but probable that the crossing might be accomplished by clinging to some part of the ships that were being locked through. Such a feat seems quite logical in light of the fact that sea snakes are air-breathing creatures with valves that close the nostrils when it is submerged. A marine fish, dependent upon a reasonably steady flow of salt water through its gills, might be expected to perish while in the fresh water. But despite all of the logical reasons to travel the short distance, the yellow-bellied sea snake seems to obediently observe the No Admittance sign set up by nature.

In some respects the family of sea snakes are seagoing cousins of the Elapidae family, which includes such deadly land snakes as the cobras, kraits, and others of their kind. This is especially true where the venom is concerned. It is fundamentally neurotoxic, attacking the nervous system as opposed to the hemotoxic venom of the pit vipers, such as the rattlers and other members of the Crotalidae family.

One peculiarity that exists in some species of sea snakes is that they possess two venomous fangs on each side of the upper jaw. They are a difficult snake to maintain in captivity, but examination of the stomach contents reveals that they feed mainly on fish. Anchovies, small mullet, and herring are apparently high on their list of favorite fish.

The fangs are similar to those of the cobra, although not quite as large as those of one of equal size. They are connected to venom glands located on either side of the head and the poison flows from the base of the fang. The pressure of the clamped jaws injects the venom into the victim's flesh.

One interesting observation exists when sea snakes are compared to many freshwater snakes and this, within itself, is somewhat of a contradiction. Many water snakes are pugnacious and quick to defend themselves by biting or striking. In contrast, the highly venomous sea snake has a reputation of being almost reluctant to bite unless it is stepped on, or otherwise roughly handled. (It should be mentioned at this point that the word *bite* is correctly used. This is true of most poisonous snakes with fixed fangs as opposed to the *strike* of the moveable fanged snakes. For example, it can be said that the coral snake bites, while a rattler strikes.)

In the family of sea snakes the average length is about four feet; some barely exceed two feet. However, at least one species attains a length of nine feet. While retaining many of the characteristics of their terrestrial relatives, some have made adaptations more suited to their marine existence. This is most noticeable in those species where the posterior portion of their bodies is flattened, with the end of the tail turning downward. This undoubtedly enables them to attain more agility in swimming.

Some species have also undergone an evolutionary change that has deprived them of the broad horizontal scales on the underside. The vertically compressed tail section and the absence of conventional belly scales have resulted in an almost total inability to glide across the ground. Exceptions are members of the genus Laticauda that have the broad abdominal scales. They range across the Indian Ocean to Africa, and while their tails are flat most of the body is round, and they move across tidal flats with ease.

Despite the difference in the underside of many species, all have body scales and possess the typical forked tongue common to land serpents. Unlike most snakes, many of which prefer to live in a restricted area, sea snakes are found in open ocean as well as the shallows near land. Many species make excursions far out to sea during the mating period.

Coloration and markings differ widely from one species to another. Many of the more venomous ones are quickly identifiable by distinct bands circling their bodies, or fingerlike stripes extending downward from the dorsal side. The yellow-bellied snake, found over the widest range, is distinct in that the back is dark, changing abruptly about halfway down the side to yellow. At the point where the tail becomes flattened, the pattern is changed so that distinct stripes appear. Some of these stripes come down from the back, while others reach up from below.

In many species the head is no larger than the neck. In others, particularly noticeable in the yellow-bellied species, the head is considerably broader and the gape of the jaws is quite pronounced. This difference indicates that these snakes feed on much larger fish than some of their relatives with smaller heads.

Sea snakes are difficult to maintain in captivity, primarily because they die of starvation. There are, of course, occasional exceptions, but most stubbornly refuse to eat. Many aquarium keepers make a special effort to provide them with seemingly ideal surroundings and supply them with a bountiful diet of the type and size fish they normally feed upon, often to no avail. This poses two problems: Prolonged studies of their habits are restricted and it also means that fresh supplies of specimens must be continually on the wanted list.

Many animals, from insects to mammals, respond favorably to captive life, thus making their habits easier for the investigator to study. Others, sea snakes included, often keep the scientist in the field for long periods and necessitate gathering odd bits and pieces of information until a comprehensive picture begins to form. Often, when a study of a large family of elusive creatures is undertaken, the observer finds that nature has handed him a jigsaw puzzle with many of the pieces not perfectly shaped and, in some cases, entirely missing. In such cases the conscientious scientist must either let years of research continue to pile up in notebooks crammed with nothing but observations or he can draw logical conclusions and label them as just that and nothing more.

The breeding and reproduction knowledge of the family of sea snakes is a classic example. With well over fifty species covering such an extensive range, and with many members overlapping the range of near and distant relatives, it becomes almost mandatory to speak in generalities.

It is known, for instance, that at times countless thousands of a specific species will congregate near the surface in open ocean hundreds of miles from land. Since at such times many have been observed in copulation, it would seem logical to conclude that certain species are, for some unexplained reason, urged to seek a pelagic environment during the mating season. It does not mean, however, that all species follow the same pattern. It is interesting to note that on occasions mating pairs have been dipped up from the ocean and they will continue the process as if they had not been disturbed.

It is known that some species are oviparous, venturing into shallow mud flats to deposit their eggs. Still others are ovoviviparous, with true eggs forming inside the female where they "hatch" and the embryonic snakelets continue to grow inside the mother's body. After a time they emerge alive, much the same as the young of the true viviparous species. The late popular naturalist Willy Ley likened ovoviviparousness to an imaginary bird that would keep an egg within its body until it hatched, subsequently giving birth to a live bird.

Still another trait contrary to many land snakes is that some species of sea snakes seem to become quite docile during their mating period. This has been observed on numerous occasions when vast numbers have been spotted far out at sea. One interesting incident brought to my personal attention was related by the pilot of a U.S. Navy PBY patrol plane on a mission out of Ceylon. He was flying low when he noticed that a wide area on the Bay of Bengal appeared to be moving with living creatures.

Examining the surface with binoculars he determined the disturbance on the otherwise calm surface was not being caused by fish. Bored by his uneventful mission, he decided to land on the water so that he might more thoroughly explore the mystery. Landing, he taxied into the squirming mass and discovered it was "millions of sea snakes." He did not know what species, but stated they were as large around as his wrist and as long as his leg. The disturbance caused by the taxiing sea plane did not seem to bother them at all.

A member of the plane's crew reached down from one of the blisters and lifted one of the snakes out of the water. It showed no inclination to bite and struggled only to get back into the sea. The only description, except for size, the pilot could give was that "they were striped with black markings." He did note that the snakes did not seem to be moving in any particular direction, but gave the impression of simply milling about in an aimless manner.

This phenomenon has frequently been observed by passengers and crew of ships far at sea. In his book, *Snake Lore* (Doubleday & Co., 1964), John Crompton relates what must have been a harrowing experience for one man.

The seaman's ship was anchored off the Pacific side of the Panama Canal and the man decided to swim ashore. He had covered about half the distance when he discovered he was surrounded by thousands of snakes. In this case the snakes appeared to be moving toward the shore. According to Crompton, the snakes were all about the swimming man, but did not seem to pay any attention to him.

It is believed that most species spend most of their lives in relatively shallow water near shore except during their seagoing voyages. Most bites are reported by net fishermen and people wading in tidal pools. There have been occasional reports of people being bitten while swimming, but those who have had extensive association with sea snakes maintain they will almost invariably attempt to move away when a swimmer or skin diver draws near.

It matters little whether the snake is peaceful or aggressive, if one does bite, the victim has been seriously injured, just the same as if he had been bitten by a cobra or a krait. Frequently, those who have been bitten and survive report there is no severe pain connected with the actual penetration of the fangs. Symptoms generally begin to develop within the first half hour.

In the early stages the victim will often complain of an aching sensation. Speech becomes steadily impaired due to an increasing paralysis of the tongue. Shortly thereafter, paralysis spreads over the entire body with lockjaw developing within a short time. The body becomes clammy, accompanied by nausea and vomiting, and respiratory difficulty is pronounced.

There are only two recommended forms of first-aid treatment and the first of these is to apply a tourniquet above the bite. It is, or should be, common knowledge that no tourniquet should remain drawn tight for more than twenty minutes. This important fact is worth repeating because in times of emotional stress some people are prone to forget some of the basic and most essential rules of first-aid treatment. After not more than twenty minutes the tourniquet should be released for several minutes, thus allowing a fresh supply of blood to flow through the injured limb. Pressure may then again be applied for another fifteen- or twenty-minute period. This should be repeated until the victim has been transported to a hospital. Leaving the tourniquet in place for a long period can result in gangrene and other serious tissue damage.

The second first-aid measure is to insist that the victim remain as inactive as possible. If there is any way to avoid it, he should not be allowed to walk. It is a far safer practice to send someone for help, even though more time may be required by such a method.

In areas where sea snakes are common hospitals generally have a supply of antivenin available. It will be of the type used to combat the venom of elapine snakes. This is a polyvalent antivenin used for the bites of several species of kraitlike snakes. It is usually effective against the venom of sea snakes when used in conjunction with general supportive care.

Because when in shallow water sea snakes make an effort to remain concealed, they will seldom be found in the vicinity of swimming beaches. Places to be avoided are areas of sluggish water such as tidal pools and stretches of coastal marshes where rocks and abundant bottom growth are present. If such areas must be traversed, a pair of knee-length rubber boots offer good protection.

One admonishment often given in the case of any snake bite is that the snake should be killed and taken with the victim to the nearest hospital so that it may be properly identified. This is unquestionably sound advice where land snakes are concerned, since it is important for the attending physician to know what type, either neurotoxic or hemotoxic, venom has been injected. In the case of a sea snake bite, however, much valuable time would likely be wasted in what could quite probably be a fruitless search. It is of more importance just to be sure it was a snake and not some other form of marine life. If the bite was from a sea snake that is really all that need be known, since the venom of all is essentially the same and there would be no question what type of antivenin should be used.

One interesting sidelight concerning snakes in the sea is that occasionally land snakes of first one type and then another will be found swimming along the surface far from shore. This usually is a result of their having been caught in a current and swept seaward, then being pushed along by a prolonged offshore wind. They can manage to stay afloat for a considerable length of time simply by keeping their lungs inflated with a sufficient amount of air. How far they may continue their unintentional voyage probably depends on how long they can avoid the jaws of a fish.

If they escape being eaten they may happen upon a piece

of driftwood. Many snakes can survive months of starvation, but unless there was some shade on their raft, they would be far more likely to succumb to the direct rays of the sun. Under favorable conditions it would be possible for a snake to drift for hundreds of miles before being eventually washed ashore.

Once while cruising nearly a hundred miles from land in the Gulf of Mexico I was on the flying bridge of our cabin boat. I was scanning the surface with binoculars for sailfish when, quite by chance, I happened to spot something moving on the smooth water some distance off the starboard bow. Curious, I put the wheel over and began steering toward it. I called to the other two fishermen onboard to train their own glasses on the object to see if they could determine what it might be.

As we drew near we saw it to be a diamondback rattlesnake about five feet long. It seemed to be unconcerned with its predicament and was contentedly floating along with its head and string of rattles held a few inches from the surface. When we were within reach one of the men hooked it with a long-handled gaff and brought it over gunwale. He let it drop to the cockpit boards and immediately the snake formed a striking coil, just as if it had been startled in its natural habitat.

Naturally, there was speculation as to why it was so far from land. It was only a guess, but we concluded it had been crossing a pass between two coastal islands and probably chose a time when the tide was on the ebb. After it was well offshore a wind had undoubtedly continued to push it farther out into the Gulf.

Rattlers are excellent swimmers for short distances but, like many large-bodied land snakes, they tire easily. This one may have elected to quit struggling to get back to land, preferring to take its chances by letting the elements move it along. Such unplanned voyages undoubtedly account for many creatures establishing permanent residence in distant parts of the world.

A similar condition may explain the presence of the

yellow-bellied sea snake in the Pacific waters along the western hemisphere. It still leaves unanswered the question of why, if one species could endure such a voyage, are there not other species that could have done the same?

6

Sharks

In that obscure time countless aeons ago, when man first began to venture into the waves that rolled in from open sea, there can be little doubt that he soon met the shark. It probably was not long before some of his fellow inhabitants were bitten, others were severely maimed, and occasionally some were killed and perhaps eaten by this fishlike creature.

This year, just as it was so long ago, the exact same scenes are being reenacted with only minor changes in the script. The most outstanding of these changes are the number of humans who are becoming victims of shark attack. Initially, it might seem logical to assume that a far greater number of those dawn men were injured or eaten. In all probability the exact reverse is true.

The logic behind such an assumption is obvious when one stops to consider the basic fact that for every one individual who ventured into the sea in those early days, there are countless thousands invading the shark's domain today. Add to this that in man's relatively brief tenure on earth, the shark population has probably remained constant. Not only are there just as many but the sharks themselves have remained physically unchanged.

Oddly enough, when a confrontation between man and shark develops, modern man is no better equipped than was his ancestor. He could never hope to outswim an attacking shark and the shark has no fear of man's weapons. Even if it were struck by a power-driven spear, a determined attack would not likely be diverted, because pain is something with which a shark is not blessed. Its dull brain simply tells it that if there is food to be had, it must continue the attack before another shark beats it to the food.

Long since relegated to the ranks of extinct animals are the saber-toothed tiger, the woolly mammoth, the great cave bear, and a host of others. Relentless hunting has reduced other large creatures to the verge of extinction. This not only applies to land animals but some of those that live in the sea, such as many of the great whales. In some cases man's greed can be blamed for the total or near-total destruction of first one species and then another. While this is undoubtedly true in some cases, it should be remembered that nature has often

Swimming shark.

Bull shark with remoras attached.

drawn the final curtain. Certainly man cannot be blamed for the disappearance of the dinosaurs, simply because they had vanished long before man made his own bid for survival.

It is as if nature is forever experimenting with various forms of life, finding some acceptable and leaving them alone, while totally rejecting another class, order, or individual species. Man is a relative newcomer to the planet Earth, but not so with the elasmobranchs that include the shark population. Probably all of the approximately three hundred species that cruise the seas of today are just as they were when man first appeared.

There is, of course, no way to know how many sharks there are, but it has been estimated that if a count could be made it would range well into the billions. The vast majority are confined to salt water as they always have been. There are three notable exceptions with the Lake Nicaragua shark, *Carcharhinus nicaraguensis*, being the most well-known freshwater species. Two others are known to live in freshwater lakes, one in Lake Izabal in Guatemala and another in New Guinea. The bull shark, *Carcharhinus leucas*, has the reputation of ranging far up into the fresh water of rivers, but is still essentially a saltwater species.

As a matter of record, sharks in general have been in the sea for a very long time. Paleontologists are convinced that sharks were among the more numerous of large sea creatures at least 300 million years ago, predating the dinosaurs by nearly a million years.

It is believed the largest carnivorous shark ever to inhabit the seas reigned supreme in the Miocene era. Today it is referred to as *Carcharodon megalodon*, and by examining the fossil teeth, many larger than a man's hand, it has been concluded that this giant measured close to fifty feet in length.

One of the most unique features of sharks is that they do not possess the typical bony skeleton common to true fish. Instead, its body frame is cartilaginous, or gristly tissue that serves to support the body the same as a true skeleton. When an animal with a true skeleton dies bacterial action soon destroys all of the body tissue, but in most cases the bones remain. Under ideal conditions the skeleton will remain for thousands of years.

Not so with sharks. The flesh disintegrates and, at a somewhat slower rate, so does the cartilaginous frame. When sufficient time has passed all that remains to be found by the casual observer will be the teeth. Actually, there would be more than just the teeth, but to the untrained eye the remains would be no more noticeable than grains of sand. These particles would be the dermal denticles that are also known as placoid teeth and compose the sandpaper surface of the shark's hide. They are similar to the hard enamel-coated teeth and serve as armor, much the same as the scales of a fish.

This shagreen, or shark hide, has for centuries been used by cabinetmakers to polish wood to a fine luster. A sheet of it will retain its abrasive properties long after many sheets of sandpaper have been worn to shreds.

These dermal denticles are so small and so closely interlocking as to go unnoticed until one feels the shark's hide. It is then that one realizes that this body surface is almost a weapon within itself. It is so abrasive that it can cause painful injury by brushing against a human's body. It can strip the paint from a boat hull and cut a heavy-test fishing line. The sharp edges of the best knives are quickly dulled when used to skin a shark of even moderate size.

Properly tanned, shark hide is extremely durable and for centuries has been used in the manufacture of luggage, shoes, belts, and numerous other articles ordinarily made of top-grain cowhide. It is a limited market, however, since processors, such as Ocean Leather Corporation of Newark, New Jersey, do not buy shark hides indiscriminately. They have their own trained suppliers who know just which species of sharks are in greatest demand and the procedure required for skinning and handling.

The shark's teeth are interesting for a number of different reasons. Obviously, the first is because they are the creature's primary weapons. Also, there is hardly such a thing as a typical shark tooth, since they come in such a wide variety of sizes and shapes. Some are long and irregularly formed; others are almost hook-shaped, curved, flattened, rough, or smooth, and many have distinctive serrations along the cutting edges. They are so unique within each species that expert marine biologists can often make a close guess as to the type of shark simply by a careful study of the wounds of a shark attack victim.

One of the most outstanding oddities where shark teeth are concerned is the rapid replacement of those that have become worn, cracked, or even broken loose from the jaw structure. It seems to make absolutely no difference how many times a shark loses a single tooth or a dozen of them; there are always replacements waiting in reserve in the jaw tissue.

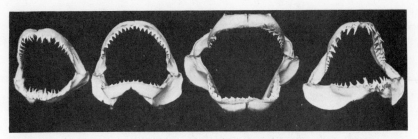

Shark jaws.

These reserve teeth lie on top of one another like the pages in a book or shingles on a roof. As soon as the active one is damaged, the replacement begins to unfold from the gum and the gap is quickly filled. Just how long this replacement process would continue is unknown, but it is generally believed it continues for the life of the shark.

When large sharks of a given species are compared with much smaller members, it will be found that each has a complete set of teeth or, if not actually perfect, any gaps are in the process of being filled by strong and healthy teeth. To further heighten this oddity is the fact that the teeth waiting to come into place are slightly larger, thus allowing the tooth size to keep pace with the increasing growth of the shark.

It is, of course, unreasonable to fancy that any animal could live forever, but sharks make a strong bid for this objective. They do not thrive in captivity, so little can be learned of their longevity from such specimens. With true fish a reasonably close approximation can be made by counting the growth rings on scales and a study of the otoliths in the inner ear. These bonelike structures are so disorganized in a shark as to be of no value and, lacking scales, establishing age can only be guesswork.

One prominent marine biologist who has conducted an extensive study of sharks for many years has made a bewildering discovery in microscopic examination of shark flesh and body organs. Even in exceptionally large sharks, he found that cell regeneration is as active as in small, and obviously young, specimens. What makes this observation so interest-

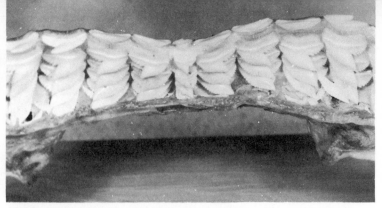

Shark jaw showing layers of reserve teeth.

ing is that senility does not begin until cell regeneration slows down or stops.

It is generally accepted that the white shark, *Carcharodon carcharias*, of the family Carcharhinidae, is an adult when it reaches a length of approximately eight feet. It is one of the most rapacious and dangerous of all sharks and is also known as the white death shark. Just because it reaches maturity at eight feet does not mean that it is nearly full grown. The largest one caught on hook and line and listed by the International Game Fish Association was sixteen feet, ten inches, and weighed 2,664 pounds. It was taken by Alfred Dean on April 21, 1959, while fishing off Ceduna in south Australian waters. In mid-August of 1975 crewmen on an oil company boat owned by the Lerner Oil Company harpooned and captured a great white shark that measured 15 feet, 2 inches and weighed 2,400 pounds. It was captured off the coast of southern California just north of Los Angeles. It was one of three large white sharks taken in the same general area in a period of two weeks.

Such sharks are, however, known to far exceed this size, so much so that Dean's shark was probably not even half grown. Reliable reports claim specimens of forty feet have been sighted and the jaws of one estimated to have measured over thirty-six feet are on display in the British Museum. Such sizes strongly suggest that the white shark closely approaches the ancient *Carcharodon megalodon* in size.

Whale sharks, *Rhincodon typus,* of forty feet are not uncommon and there are numerous verified accounts of even much larger ones having been harpooned and held long enough for an approximate measurement to be made by comparing these giants to the known length of the ships participating in the harpooning.

For all practical purposes, whale sharks are true sharks, but they differ for two significant reasons. The first is that they are quite likely the largest members of the entire clan and secondly, under no circumstances can they be considered man-eaters. The reason for the latter is that, despite their size, their diet consists solely of plankton and very small school fish which they swallow in vast quantities. They have a small gullet and no teeth capable of ripping or tearing flesh of larger creatures.

In direct contrast where size is concerned, the smallest of all sharks is *Squaliolus laticaudus,* found in the western

White shark.

World's record white shark, caught by Alfred Dean.

140

Pacific. It measures only about half a foot in length and is so rare that it does not have a common name.

Since we are conditioned to believe that all animals must be restricted to some approximate life-span, it is interesting to speculate on that of the shark. Naturally many of them are mortally wounded in the often fierce competition for food. When such an event occurs the injured member stands little chance, because most sharks are cannibalistic and a severely wounded one would quickly fall prey to its own kind. It is also well known that if the opportunity presents itself, a large shark will not hesitate to eat any smaller shark it can catch.

There are still other oddities concerning these creatures that undoubtedly contribute to their longevity. Cancer, for example, is unknown in sharks, and there is a growing suspicion that heart disease is almost nonexistent. Several human health institutions about the world are currently engaged in extensive studies in an effort to discover what natural protection exists in shark anatomy to resist these diseases. It would, indeed, be an ironic twist of fate if man's age-old enemy of the sea eventually led science to a cure or immunization to protect humans from these two killers.

It might be assumed that the cause of eventual shark mortality would be that it simply grows too large to capture enough food to sustain life. Yet, with growth comes increased speed and strength and, since a shark is decidedly nonselective in its diet, it could remain well fed by capturing a wide assortment of underwater life. Squid, alone, are present in such vast numbers in the sea that just that one creature would provide a virtually inexhaustible food supply.

If it were not for one outstanding difference in a shark's anatomy, when compared to many true fishes, dead ones might be found floating on the surface and science could conduct postmortem examinations, thus reaching some conclusion as to the cause of death. Unlike many fishes, however, the shark has no swim bladder and, lacking this natural flotation, it sinks to the bottom when it stops swimming. The large ones that might provide the answer probably sink in deep water where their bodies soon begin to decay and provide food for lowly forms of scavengers.

The absence of the swim bladder undoubtedly presents a problem for the shark because many of the active species must stay on the move almost constantly. It is of vital importance to the shark's existence because it is only by moving forward that sufficient water is taken in through the mouth so that oxygen can be extracted by the gills.

Most fish, whether it be the common freshwater sunfish or the great barracuda, inflate this bladder with just enough air to enable them to maintain a natural buoyancy. By doing so they can remain suspended at a selected depth and rest for a desired period of time, taking in oxygen-supplying water simply by opening and shutting the jaws. The only rest offered to many species of sharks is to stop swimming and gradually sink toward the bottom so that the gliding movement will force the required amount of water through the mouth and across the gills.

Some shark species have a slower metabolism that does not require much oxygen and they can survive quite well by resting on the bottom for long periods. Some of the more active ones will occasionally be seen lying almost motionless on the bottom for brief periods, but even then it must position itself in a spot where a natural current of water, such as the steady flow of the tide, affords a suitable intake of water.

One of the most perplexing mysteries concerning sharks I have ever encountered was observed a few years ago along the west coast of Florida. My wife and I had been fishing most of the day and as we were returning I was standing in the bow of our open boat. When we were about a quarter of a mile from shore I caught sight of a hammerhead shark, *Sphyrna mokarran*, lying motionless on the bottom. The water was exceptionally clear and there was no difficulty in making an accurate identification. This, within itself, was no real accomplishment, since this species of hammerhead is one of the most easily recognized of all sharks because of its abnormal head shape.

Calling to my wife, who was steering at the time, I told her to slow the boat and circle the area. When I again spotted the shark I signaled, she cut the engine, and we began drifting.

Hammerhead shark.

Much to my bewilderment, there was not one, but a total of twenty-five hammerheads, all dead and ranging in size from about seven feet on down to a few barely two feet in length. As we drifted about we became aware of still another puzzling fact in that all of the dead sharks were scattered helter-skelter over an area of not more than one acre.

Completely baffled at the strange discovery, I quickly tied a weighted snatch hook to a length of heavy line and began hoisting one shark after another to the surface. This only served to heighten the mystery even more, because we found that each had a deep gash in the area between the wide head and the gill slits. In a few cases the nearly identical cuts were present on both the right and left sides. There were no other signs of injury and the wounds were certainly not deep enough to have brought about death so suddenly that all would have died in the immediate area.

I knew that sharks, especially small ones, occasionally fall victim to the so-called red tide. This phenomenon is caused by a rapid proliferation of a microorganism known as *Gymnodinium breve* that causes widespread destruction of animal life that depends on gills for breathing. This possibility was immediately ruled out because it had been well over a year since this plague had been present in the local waters.

I was acquainted with most of the commercial fishermen in the area and on the following day I began contacting them to find if any could offer an explanation. We returned to the spot several times in the next few days and the sharks were still there, but no one could suggest a plausible answer.

Anyone reasonably knowledgeable concerning the habits of the hammerhead knows they do not travel in family groups. Furthermore, the local fishermen would have known if any members of their trade had trapped such a large number in a net. Even then, they would have been hard pressed to hold that many sharks and systematically slaughter each in the same manner.

The discovery still remains as much of a mystery now as on the day my wife and I examined the sharks. I have discussed the subject in detail with several marine biologists and none has been able to suggest a reasonable answer. As I continued to visit the area for several days another observation was made. As the process of decay advanced, all of the sharks remained on the bottom. Before a period of inclement weather brought a halt to my visits I noticed that large numbers of crown conchs, *Melongena corona,* had collected and were gradually devouring the carcasses. Although these conchs are carnivores, normally feeding on other shellfish, they seemed attracted to the dead sharks.

One of the incongruities of shark feeding habits is that, while they will eat virtually anything, including members of their own kind, they are repelled by the decaying flesh of other sharks. When in a feeding frenzy they will fight to tear chunks out of wounded members. However, if one is killed and kept until it begins to decay and then returned to the water no shark will attempt to eat it and, in fact, shy away

Shark feeding on fish.

from it. What makes this interesting is that, with the exception of decaying sharks, these creatures that are often referred to as swimming garbage cans will show no hesitation at eating any other type of flesh with little or no regard for the degree of putrification.

A shark is undoubtedly the most nonselective feeder that lives. It will eat anything it can swallow and if the object is too large it utilizes its powerful jaws and sharp teeth to rip away large chunks. Possibly the largest recorded single item found in a shark's stomach was the carcass of an entire reindeer taken from a large specimen of a Greenland shark, *Somniosus microcephalus*. This species is known to reach a length of twenty-four feet and was long prized for the high content of oil found in its liver. The Greenland shark that yielded the body of the reindeer had been harpooned by the crew of a whaling ship.

Examination of the contents of any large shark's stomach is a repulsive task, but seldom fails to produce an interesting and often almost unbelievable collection of articles that even a shark could not digest. Once while on a merchant ship we hooked and brought aboard a large blue shark, *Prionace glauca*. When we were certain it was dead we allowed several interested members of the crew to empty its stomach on the deck. Along with an evil-smelling mass of partly digested fish and garbage, well over two dozen indigestible articles were counted. Included were such items as an aluminum soup kettle, a carpenter's square, a plastic cigar box, a jar of nails, a flashlight, a length of quarter-inch nylon line, a rubber raincoat, a rubber-soled shoe, tin cans, glass bottles, and a roll of tar paper. The latter was three feet wide and when unrolled was found to be twenty-seven feet long.

The above assortment was by no means unusual. Examination of numerous other sharks has proven that at one time or another they are likely to grab anything that is thrown or falls from a ship. Such items as boots, tin cans, chunks of wood, or anything is likely to be swallowed when the competition with other sharks is keen. The shark sees an object hit the water and makes a quick rush to grab it before it is taken by another.

As was stated, the most unusual collection of items swallowed by sharks are articles that fall or are thrown from the decks of ships. This is primarily so because numerous sharks are predominantly pelagic and often follow ships for days at a time, apparently having discovered that considerable quantities of garbage are periodically jettisoned. Examples of these oceanic species are the blue, white, and mako, but there are many others.

It should be emphasized that while certain types will often be found far at sea, they are not restricted to open ocean and will move in very close to shore. It is known that certain species, such as the nurse sharks and bull sharks and others that spend much of their time in shallow bays and inlets, are less prone to swallow foreign objects. This is probably because they are normally slow-swimming species and more likely to investigate an unfamiliar object before eating it.

Rarely does swallowing indigestible objects cause the shark any trouble. When the accumulation reaches a point where it impedes its swimming ability, it simply regurgitates the excess baggage and makes a fresh start. It was long believed that the digestive juices of these creatures were so caustic that they would dissolve almost anything. Chemical analysis, however, has disproved this and it has been established that the fluids secreted by a shark's stomach do not differ to any appreciable extent from those of fish or mammals. Hydrochloric acid is necessary for the effective action of the proteolytic enzyme. Shark pepsin, as the enzyme is commonly known, does show a minor difference from similar stomach acids of other animals in that it is effective at considerably lower temperatures.

Even were it not for man, with his steadily mounting flow of garbage and other organic wastes heedlessly dumped into the sea, the shark's diet would still be wide and varied. It is forever on the lookout for almost every form of food the sea has to offer. Fish, turtles, octopuses, squid, crabs, morays, porpoise, and rays are but a few examples, and sharks will even take sea birds that might be resting on the surface or diving for fish.

It is reasonably well established that sharks are insensitive to pain. Numerous species feed extensively on stingrays and it is not at all uncommon to capture a specimen with dozens of the venomous spines from the rays imbedded in the area surrounding the mouth. On occasions, when a shark manages to catch a large moray moving from one hiding spot to another, it will unhesitatingly grab it, apparently oblivious to the injury, even inside the mouth, inflicted by the powerful tooth-studded jaws of the moray.

On frequent occasions, most often noticed in the so-called mob feeding pattern, a shark will be disemboweled by a larger and more powerful companion. At such times it is not unusual for the mortally wounded shark to eat its own trailing intestinal organs. This has been observed countless times in the early days of whaling. When the blubber was being flensed alongside the whaling ship, sharks often gathered in large numbers. Frequently, an irate flenser would split a shark open with his long-handled blubber lance and watch as the hunger-crazed shark cannibalized the contents of its own body. In such cases the injured shark seldom had an opportunity to continue his autophagous feast for long, because it was usually torn apart and eaten by other sharks in the mob.

Almost everyone can recall seeing at least one movie when the dauntless hero was called upon to fight it out with a large shark. Such sequences usually concluded with the man plunging his knife into the shark and the vanquished beast sank away into the depths, leaving behind a trail of blood. In real life, this would seldom work because the wound, excepting a direct penetration of the brain, would have little immediate effect on a shark if it were actively engaged in a fight for food. If the wound were severe enough the shark might possibly die later on because of internal bleeding, but at the moment it would hardly deter a determined attack.

A shark is, in fact, one of the most difficult of all dangerous animals to kill quickly. The only sure way is to destroy the brain, as might be done with a shot from a gun. Even then, it would be more a matter of luck, rather than marksmanship, because the brain is small and if it were missed by only a few inches the shark would still remain functional for some time.

An effective weapon has been designed that consists of a short tube at the end of a long handle. The tube is loaded with a shotgun shell that is discharged by a firing pin fitted in the end of the handle. When forcefully rammed against an object, such as a shark's head, the pin strikes the cap in the shell causing it to fire. To be immediately effective, however, it must destroy the shark's head or sufficiently shatter its body. At such point-blank range the shock wave will stun it so that it is rendered helpless. Despite its efficiency, such a weapon should be used only by someone skilled in its operation.

Shark churning water at surface.

On one memorable occasion we battled a twelve-foot white shark for well over an hour and when it seemed to be subdued it was shot in the head with a 30-30 rifle. It shuddered and immediately became motionless. The hook was removed and rebaited as the seemingly lifeless creature drifted downward. Fifteen minutes later there was another strike followed by a twenty-minute struggle. When it was brought alongside we discovered it was the same shark, with blood still seeping from the bullet hole.

The above should not be interpreted as typical of shark behavior, but only as an example of how they will occasionally react. Often an aggressive shark can be driven away by being struck with the blade of an oar. Again, they will give every indication of intended attack, only to suddenly swim away of their own free will.

As frightening as it may seem to some, I think it would be safe to say that annually countless numbers of surf bathers are paced and observed by one or more sharks that eventually turn away without ever being seen by the possible human target. One common belief is that a shark approaching a swimmer will cruise close to the surface so that its dorsal fin will be seen cleaving the surface. Some do, but many others carry out their reconnoitering well below the surface and, having satisfied their curiosity, move on without ever being seen. If every shark that approached a swimmer decided to attack, this popular form of recreation would have been abandoned long ago.

It is of interest to note that the word "shark" did not enter the vocabulary for a very long time. For thousands of years they were mentioned in writing as "monsters" by some, while others called them "dogfish." It is believed that the name shark was made part of the English language as recently as the middle of the sixteenth century, when an English sea captain put a large specimen on display in London. Some lexicographers believe the word *schurke* came from the German language where it meant scoundrel or villain, and was applied to these creatures because of their unpleasant nature.

Whenever the subject of sharks becomes the topic of conversation someone is sure to ask the oft repeated question, "What are the chances of being attacked by a shark while swimming at a popular beach?" When someone who has made a study of the subject replies with the statement that the odds are probably one in several million, there is almost sure to be disagreement. The usual argument against such a loose statistical answer involves the not-infrequent newspaper accounts that relate the details of a recent attack off the coast of Florida, California, New Jersey, and numerous other locations. It is usually added that this is not taking into account attacks in other parts of the world.

What the advocate of the supposed shark menace overlooks is that in between these reports of attacks, countless millions of people have gone for a dip in the briny without encountering a shark. The odds still stand, but it is pointless to deny that each year a number of people are either killed or severely injured by sharks. To that very small minority statistics, odds and percentages are of little consequence, but in the overall picture the actual danger is often grossly exaggerated.

The fear of being attacked by a shark demonstrates one of the incongruities of the human fear of death or injury. The same person who has a morbid dread of becoming a shark victim, seldom displays more than the mildest concern for his safety while traveling along the highway in his automobile.

Automobile accidents are so numerous as to have become almost an accepted way of being killed or injured. Unless the wreck is so spectacular and involves a large number of people, only the local newspapers will bother to provide space for the account. If, on the other hand, a person is killed or severely mauled by a shark most editors will often give it full coverage, even though it may have happened at some distant place. It is not a misplaced sense of value on the part of the editor. Instead, he knows that an account of a shark attack arouses reader interest far more than would a commonplace accident report.

No one has ever satisfactorily been able to explain why humans will unhesitatingly expose themselves to countless other dangers, yet shudder at the thought of being eaten by a shark. Such an abnormal fear was forcefully brought to public attention during World War II. Anyone on a ship or flying over the ocean in hostile areas was always in danger from enemy action. It was tragic enough that so many had to die from torpedoes, bombs, and gunfire, but the thought that some might become shark victims piqued public opinion to the point of demanding that something be done to prevent it.

The result was that on December 6, 1942, a year after the Japanese attack on Pearl Harbor, a crash program was put into effect to find and develop an effective shark repellent. Those most concerned were the United States Navy, Air Force, and War Shipping Administration. Any and all scientists who had done serious research on sharks were urged to participate. Also invited were nonscientists who had extensive experience with sharks. This included well-known sporting anglers and those who fished for sharks commercially.

Many experiments were conducted at Woods Hole Oceanographic Institution in Massachusetts, but the work and tests were not confined to sharks in captive tanks. Investigations were conducted at far-flung locations where sharks could be expected to be found in the largest concentrations. One of the primary field testing grounds was the Gulf of Guayaquil along the coast of Ecuador, selected because it was known to possess an abundance of numerous species of sharks on a year-round basis.

No reasonable scheme suggested from any scientific field was spurned. Numerous electronic attempts were tried to no avail. Rotenone, long known as an effective fish poison, was tried. It killed and temporarily incapacitated fish in large numbers, but had little or no effect on sharks. It was hurriedly dismissed. The fish it killed or stunned actually attracted sharks to the area where they might not normally have congregated and sent many of the sharks into a feeding frenzy.

Stewart Springer, the senior scientist connected with the urgent program, had been chosen for the position because of his undisputed authority on shark taxonomy, as well as their behavior under a wide variety of conditions. It was through his efforts and knowledge that the project eventually approached anything resembling an effective shark repellent.

Aware of a shark's aversion to decaying shark flesh, Springer and those with him concentrated on this clue. Extensive experiments proved that the body of a decaying shark would not only remain untouched by other sharks but it was discovered that many sharks would leave the vicinity as soon as they sensed the carcass.

At the time, shark fishing was a thriving enterprise, with the hides being used for leather, the flesh for supplements for animal food, and the vitamin-rich livers being rendered for medicinal purposes. One of the largest headquarters for commercial shark fishing was at the Florida town of Salerno, and it was there that chemists began the task of trying to analyze the elements of decaying shark flesh.

Excitement ran high when it was discovered that when ammonium acetate was separated and applied to otherwise desirable shark bait it was spurned. Two other elements, out of a total of seventy-eight elements tested, proved to have some repellent value. These were maleic acid and copper sulphate. But the most valuable appeared to be ammonium acetate which, when dissolved in seawater, produced acetic acid. The eventual combination was copper acetate crystals. When packed in a porous bag, the chemical dissolved at a rate of about a quarter of a pound per hour.

When attached to a line close to a suitable bait sharks would leave the chemically clouded bait alone. Controls con-sisted of three lines baited the same, but two were left un-

Boatload of commercially caught sharks.

treated. There was considerable action on the "clear" lines, but relatively none on the one with the repellent.

Taking into consideration that squid and octopuses are natural prey of sharks and that they often escape by discharging their ink which confuses the shark, experimenters elected to capitalize on this. As a result, the Calco Chemical Division of the American Cyanamid Company produced a nigrosine-type dye that dissolved quickly and effectively clouded the water. This was added to the copper acetate.

So that search planes might stand a better chance of spotting floating survivors, a fluorescent dye that covered the surface with a bright color was added to the concoction. The surface dye, the artificial cephalopod ink crystals, and the copper acetate were compressed into a six-and-a-half-ounce cake and packaged in a waterproof container pouch. It would remain intact until the survivors of a sea disaster found themselves in shark-infested waters. It could then be ripped open and supposedly repel any and all sharks. The packet was labeled Shark Chaser.

From a psychological standpoint, Shark Chaser served an important role in bolstering the morale of men who were likely to find themselves adrift in lifejackets or on a survival raft. It was standard equipment for personnel who would be traveling on or over waters forty-five degrees on either side of the equator. The scientists who had developed it, however, were far from satisfied. Experiments had proven that, at best, it was about 50 percent effective against shark attack.

True, it would deter a cruising shark if it entered the area from down current, but it had no effect on another shark homing in from the opposite direction. Added to this, if a shark did make an attack and blood began to spill out into the water, other sharks followed the stronger urge to feed and paid little attention to the repellent. How many lives it may have saved can only be a matter of conjecture, but the fact that it was at least partially effective was better than nothing at all.

With the cessation of hostilities experiments continued in the search for a more effective repellent. At this writing the most promising approach seems to lie in the electronic field.

It has been discovered that if an electrical current produced by a battery pack is switched on, approaching sharks will shy away. Logically, the current is not strong enough to harm the wearer, although he is aware of it. If a unit employing this principle can be made small enough to be comfortably worn by an individual it may prove to be the answer to a problem that has long baffled countless research scientists.

Still another device that shows promise in helping to protect survivors of sea disasters is a baglike container known as Shark Screen. It is about six feet in length and deep enough to allow a man to stand upright in it. At the top is a flotation raft that keeps the bag and survivor afloat. Experiments have been favorable, probably because the odor of the human is contained within the bag and the enclosure does not permit the occupant's arms and legs to dangle. It is believed that such waving targets often encourage sharks to make an experimental bite. Such a piece of equipment, however, would be restricted to survival use, since it would not be practical for swimmers and skin divers.

Australia and the east coast of Africa probably have the highest incidence of recorded shark attacks of any places in the world. Fencing off long strips of desirable swimming

Navy doctors working on shark-bitten foot.

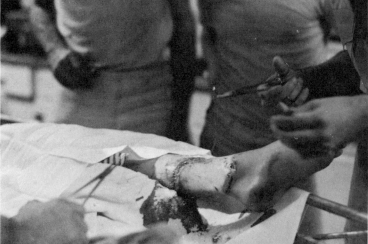

areas has been tried with some measure of success. The problem has always been the initial cost and the continuing expense of inspecting and maintaining such fences. More recently strips of nets with wide mesh have been substituted, on the theory that beach-bound sharks would become entangled.

This method is considerably less costly and countless sharks have been trapped in the dangling net screens, but since the mesh does not enclose the entire area, occasional sharks do get through and attack swimmers. When the shark does become entangled it is prevented from swimming and this in turn brings about its death due to oxygen deprivation.

Popular resort areas in the United States, as well as other countries, have resorted to numerous defense measures. One of these was called the "bubble fence" which consisted of long lengths of perforated pipe placed on the bottom. Air was pumped into the pipes and the bubbles came out of the numerous holes. It proved quite effective on captive sharks in pens and tanks, but under actual conditions the cost factor again had to be considered. They required frequent cleaning to remove shell growth that clogged the holes. Added to this, there was never any positive proof that large, aggressive sharks were sufficiently frightened.

Air patrol, using both light planes and blimps, offers limited warning, since conditions for spotting a shark are not always ideal. The aircraft, which is equipped with large bull horns to sound the warning, cannot visually cover the entire area, and a hungry shark could slip by unnoticed. Tall towers, manned by competent observers, are in use at certain beaches and, likè the aircraft observer, the tower watcher can spot a shark if sunlight and other conditions are good. If it happens to be a cloudy day, or one when long foam-crested combers are rolling shoreward, again the potentially dangerous shark can avoid detection.

Still another question frequently asked is "Which sharks are most likely to attack a human swimmer?" A few years ago many marine biologists who had made a study of the subject were likely to respond with a list of a dozen or so that established a bad reputation. Now, with the number of people who enter the sea increasing rapidly, many sharks that were once considered completely harmless have been added to this list. One widely recognized authority on sharks flatly refused to count off any certain species, preferring to rely on actual proof by saying: "The big ones and the little ones."

At first this may seem facetious, but the records show that sharks as small as two and a half feet in length have been responsible for painful and unprovoked attacks on swimmers. It is generally agreed that the white shark, *Carcharodon carcharias*, leads the list of sharks known to be man-eaters. Records prove, however, that it has several other contenders vying for the title. The lemon shark, *Negaprion brevirostris*, for example, is an inshore shark and one with a pugnacious temperament. Its attitude and the fact that it frequents waters where large numbers of humans are likely to be swimming make it necessary to add it to the list.

Hardly a year passes that documented reports fail to add still another species to the "established" list of proven man-eaters or those making injurious attacks. In the past thirty years this list has nearly tripled in length, and numerous others are being more seriously considered as possible suspects.

Special conditions often dictate the potential danger of certain species. Some are primarily oceanic, thus making them decidedly more dangerous to survivors of sea disasters, but, as previously mentioned, many of these forsake their pelagic existence and patrol inshore waters from time to time.

For some unexplained reason some seem to give up their far-ranging habits and even desert others of their kind to take up residence in a bay or lagoon. These bank loafers, as they are generally known, are suspected of being responsible for many of the attacks on humans.

The reason, many believe, these rogue sharks may be more dangerous than others of their kind is that for some reason they may not be able to catch a sufficient number of fish and other forms of sea life to satisfy their appetites. It is also suspected that because they remain in a relatively restricted area they have had ample opportunity to observe people and have concluded they do not represent a threat to their safety.

There are several logical reasons why a shark may institute what is generally termed an unprovoked attack on swimmers. The first concerns any large shark that chances upon a human who may have fallen from the deck of a ship, for example. In such a situation the shark has an opportunity to observe the person as he attempts to stay afloat. It seems an easy target and if it makes the attack and spills blood, there is almost no reason for it to fail to complete its mission.

Again, there may be other sharks nearby and all may be feeding on fish. Here, the spirit of competition enters the picture. This is always dangerous because a shark's survival depends on being the first one to grab a bite. In still another situation one or more swimmers may be frolicking in the water. To any nearby shark, this may be viewed as some injured creature and such is an open invitation to a shark. Then there is always the possibility that the shark is hungry and is simply ready to tackle anything it thinks it can capture.

In any of the above situations there is little doubt that the attacks would be anything but deliberate. A porpoise, seal, or fish would suffer the same fate. It is believed, however, that the majority of shark attacks, especially those in relatively shallow water, are a result of mistaken identity.

A shark, either a bank loafer or one that has just cruised shoreward out of curiosity, may be trailing a school of fish or searching for rays. He and the human may pass close to one another and the shark may only catch sight of a hand or foot. This is particularly true when the water is cloudy with roiled bottom sand or when large waves are cresting. To the shark, the hand or foot may appear at the instant as a single small creature similar to the type of food it has been pursuing.

At the sight of the moving object the shark's instinct tells it to grab the object before it gets away. The instant its jaws clamp shut the human has been injured, because a shark's jaws are exceedingly strong. Dr. Perry W. Gilbert has conducted extensive experiments on the power of a shark's jaws. One of his tests involved an eight-and-one-half-foot dusky shark, *Carcharhinus obscurus,* and, using specially designed equipment, he was able to accurately measure the crushing

White shark, jaws open at surface.

power of this common- and medium-sized shark's jaws. The results showed that the clamping power was not to be measured in pounds, but in tons per square inch of biting surface. Such extreme pressure can snap an arm or leg bone with the ease of a person breaking a pencil.

Logically, if the shark in question exerted full pressure on the first bite, the human would lose whatever part of his anatomy that was in the shark's mouth. Often, especially when a shark is unsure of what it is biting, it will make an exploratory grab. At this point one of several courses may develop. The shark may be startled when it becomes aware that it has clamped its jaws on something much larger than originally believed. Puzzled, it may let go and cruise off some distance to ponder the situation.

If that happens the injured swimmer may have an opportunity to reach the safety of the beach before the flow of blood stimulates the shark's appetite to the extent that it is provoked to another attack. If again, the shark is of a more stubborn nature it may decide to grab again and hang on, or it may even decide to hold the first bite. One example of such tenacity occurred on July 27, 1958, at 4:10 P.M. and resulted in the loss of a leg for an eight-year-old boy.

At the time, Douglas Lawton and his twelve-year-old brother were splashing about in shallow water about ten feet from shore on the Gulf side of Longboat Key near Sarasota, Florida. It is a popular swimming area and as the Lawton boys played, they were watched by their parents and an aunt and uncle. Suddenly, Douglas screamed and as the horrified adults raced down the beach they saw the boy fighting to keep his head above water.

The older brother reached him only seconds before the adults raced out to his rescue. Blood was gushing into the water and all saw a shark slightly over five feet in length clinging onto the youngster's left thigh. Amid all of the confusion, with a total of five people helping, the shark held on with determination. As they dragged the boy ashore they repeatedly beat and pounded the shark and the father grabbed the shark's body and struggled in a desperate effort to dislodge it.

As quickly as it had made the attack, the shark released its grip and darted off into deeper water. Young Lawton was rushed to the nearest hospital. The attending physicians had no choice but to complete the job the shark had begun. The leg was removed just below the hip.

Dr. Eugenie Clark, who was at the time director of the nearby Cape Haze Marine Experiment Station and an expert on sharks, conducted an extensive investigation by questioning the rescuers and examining the wound. Her conclusion was that the attack had been made by a young tiger shark, *Galeocerdo cuvier.*

Still another condition that occasionally stems from what began as an accidental or unprovoked bite concerns the possibility that the shark may be accompanied by additional sharks. Blood is spilled by the shark making the attack and

Tiger shark, swimming.

the scent is swiftly detected by one of its companions. Seldom is the victim, or those around him, calm enough to view the situation from an analytical standpoint. All they may know is that a shark has bitten a human. In the terrifying minutes that follow, the victim and those around him may not realize that what appears to be another attack by the same shark may, in reality, be an entirely different shark. Another and still another may dart in for a bite. In such a case one person may say it was a four-foot shark, another may be positive it was a six-footer, and so on. In reality, all may be accurate, with the confusing reports stemming from the fact that there was more than one shark involved.

A combination of blood in the water and the frantic movements of a wounded victim, human or otherwise, create a deadly situation if several sharks are nearby. They are creatures that act on impulse and their instinct is to rush into the fray to get as much food as they can before it is devoured by their companions. At such times caution or wariness is ignored and they rush at the target with fury matched by few other groups of animals.

Numerous tests have been conducted and carefully observed to study this form of attack that is known as the mob feeding pattern. In such experiments the investigators lure as many sharks as possible by the use of chum. When they are milling around, feeding on fish scraps or offal, a large quantity of similar food is suddenly dumped overboard. It can be predicted with near certainty that the frantic behavior will begin. Once the mob feeding is in full swing the sharks will grab anything that is tossed into the melee. The objects can range from chunks of lumber to broken bottles and they will even fight savagely for possession of something as inedible as an old tire.

One fallacy that is widespread and firmly believed by many is that if a school of porpoise is sighted, the area is sure to be clear of sharks. It makes a good tale, but quite often the exact reverse is true. It is true that many sharks are wary of a school of porpoise, but they will trail along behind them for two reasons.

Sharks in "mob feeding pattern."

The possibility of catching a porpoise pup is one reason sharks will follow the mammals. The second is that the shark knows the porpoise is a gluttonous feeder and also wasteful. The porpoise will pursue a large school of fish and when it grabs one, if the whole fish is not in its mouth, the head or the tail is cut off and sinks to the bottom. The porpoise gives the impression that it enjoys the chase and it is too skilled a hunter to waste time circling around picking up the pieces. This is ideal for the trailing sharks and they can count on ample food simply by picking up the scraps.

Porpoises are powerful and swift-swimming animals, and they will band together if a shark threatens the safety of any of their members, especially the young. They can easily match, and often exceed, the speed of any shark. Their method of fighting a shark is to rush at it and butt it with powerful blows by using their heads as battering rams.

A lone shark that causes trouble for a herd will beat a hasty retreat. If it fails to escape, one porpoise after another will bore in, striking it with so many sledgehammer blows that its

Two porpoises.

internal organs will be so severely ruptured that it can no longer continue swimming. Conversely, if a large shark happens upon a lone porpoise it will catch and make a meal of this popular mammal.

Like human children, porpoise pups have to be watched because they have a tendency to stray off and go exploring on their own. The adult porpoises know this and so do the sharks. If one of the youngsters falls behind, or wanders too far afield, a shark of sufficient size is quite likely just waiting to grab the pup if it feels it can do so without a retaliatory attack. Intelligent creatures that they are, however, the porpoise herd is generally on guard for such an eventuality and apparently makes an effort to keep their pups in range and away from possible danger.

Because people have occasionally seen a herd of porpoise killing a shark, the myth that they seek and destroy sharks has grown. Those who have made a serious study of these two entirely different creatures will leave the surf if they catch sight of feeding porpoise approaching. It has been demonstrated countless times that the most productive shark fishing is in the wake of a porpoise herd.

There seems to exist a sort of truce between porpoise and sharks. As long as the shark does not become aggressive it will not be bothered. It is not that the porpoise do not know they are being trailed by one or more sharks. They apparently do not care, as long as the sharks remain behind at a discreet distance.

Still another standard question that is often asked is: "Do sharks ever become confirmed man-eaters?" If the intent of the question is to ask if there are any sharks that feed exclusively on people, the answer is no. If, for example, a large shark grew to depend on human bodies for the bulk of its food, it would hardly be satisfied with less than one every week or so. No known coastline where records are kept has ever reported such a loss of life to sharks.

If, on the other hand, the question is intended to mean whether or not an individual shark may attack more than one person in a short period of time, any truthful answer must be obscure and punctuated with probabilities and possibilities.

It is entirely within reason to believe a shark may attack and eat a human and continue on with its normal diet for a while before making another attack on a human. A possible exception might be if a series of frequent attacks were made in a restricted area and there were enough qualified witnesses to make a positive identification. However, such a condition would hardly ever be possible from a scientific point of view. Here is a first-rate example of how what seems to be little more than folklore can be true fact, but could hardly be proven.

A small island village may have as its focal point a small lagoon. Many of the villagers may clearly recall a time when a large shark with some distinguishing feature, such as a missing fin or a pronounced scar, caused trouble over a period of time. If fishing happened to be an important part of the town's livelihood, the inhabitants might well remember seeing that particular shark attack one of the inhabitants. If it returned again and again and made other attacks, the people would logically be convinced it was a confirmed man-eater. If the story were eventually relayed to a scientific research panel, it could be accepted only as an account told by a number of people, but there would always be the element of doubt. The practical investigator could not be certain whether the same shark was responsible for all attacks, or whether a number of sharks were involved. The power of suggestion might have caused the inhabitants to accept one another's excited report.

The most frequently repeated story that suggests that on rare occasions an individual shark might find human swimmers an easy target began on July 2, 1916, at Beach Haven, New Jersey. On what was to be the first of five successive attacks, a twenty-four-year-old man was grabbed by a shark and so much flesh was torn from one of his legs that he died in a matter of hours from loss of blood. Only four days later, and thirty-five miles north at Spring Lake, New Jersey, a second man lost part of one leg and both feet. He, too, died as a result of shark attack. On July 12, thirty miles north of Spring Lake, at Matawan, New Jersey, there were three more attacks in the same day and two of these were fatal. A man attempted to rescue a boy that was being attacked by a shark. As he was carrying the youngster ashore, he was also attacked. Both died as a result. Later that same afternoon only a few miles away a boy was attacked and one of his legs was stripped of so much flesh that what remained had to be amputated.

Thus, in a space of ten days five people had been attacked, four had died, and one had lost a leg. All had been in areas where swimming was commonly enjoyed and the distance between the first and the last was less than a hundred miles. Two weeks after the first attack an eight-foot, six-inch white shark was caught in Raritan Bay a few miles farther north. When the stomach was opened it was found to contain fifteen pounds of human flesh and the bones matched the remains of the second victim.

Witnesses were reasonably consistent when reporting the size of the shark involved in each attack and it coincided with the one caught in Raritan Bay. That, combined with the human remains found in the stomach, suggests that all attacks might have been made by the same shark.

It is entirely possible that all attacks were made by the same shark. Those who saw the man attempting to rescue the boy in Matawan Creek were sure those two attacks were made by the same shark. The one that contained the missing bones of the July 6 victim was unquestionably the same animal. The other attacks, no matter how logical it is to believe, can only be conjecture. Although their size reports were close, some people saw one attack while others witnessed others, but none could report any outstanding features about the shark—or sharks—they saw.

It is reasonable to assume that once a shark has made an attack on a human it may lose any caution which might otherwise make it wary of this alien creature. Once it has discovered a human is so easily overpowered, it might even be inclined to attack the next time an opportunity presented itself. This, however, is giving a shark credit for having a better memory than is suspected.

One fact that has been fairly well established is that the frequency of shark attacks along a given stretch of coastline will increase every few years and then either taper off or stop

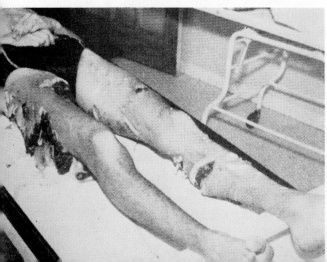

Mutilated human body—shark attack.

abruptly. One interesting theory that may have a bearing on this is that ocean currents occasionally waver from their normal route. Both commercial and sport fishermen are aware that one year a particular type of migratory fish is to be found much closer to shore than in other years. Since it is known that many species of sharks follow migrating fish, it is logical to conclude that when vast numbers of fish are close in, so will be the sharks. With more sharks in a vicinity frequented by swimmers, the chance of an occasional attack automatically increases.

But such is only speculation and it would require years of comprehensive study to establish the validity of such a theory. Many factors would have to be considered and no positive conclusion could be reached in a hurry-up program. Then, to cloud such a study, is the decidedly unpredictable nature of all sharks. Their behavior is rife with contradictions.

As previously mentioned, the general public became increasingly shark-conscious during World War II and an ever-increasing number of marine biologists have begun to specialize in the taxonomy, distribution, and behavior of sharks. One fact has begun to emerge and that is the number of shark attacks has been increasing in recent years. At this point, the serious student should be hesitant to conclude that the number of sharks is growing, or that they are becoming more aggressive.

The two important factors that must be taken into consideration are that the number of people frequenting the sea is growing rapidly. Also, better records are kept by interested scientific organizations. The latter is by no means a simple task because, whether they are willing to admit it or not, seaside resorts are generally reluctant to publicize any trouble with sharks. Fortunately, few newspapers will squelch such news, but there are times when the reporters are confronted with stone walls when they try to get the true story. Then, again, if the victim is eaten by a shark or sharks and the event is not witnessed by reasonably dependable observers, the swimmer who is listed as missing cannot be said with certainty to have been lost to sharks.

One interesting sidelight in connection with the possibility of shark attacks was voiced by the chief lifeguard at a popular California beach. This man, with years of experience in protecting human life, stated that, in his considered opinion, about half of the reported drownings, in which no body was recovered, were due to shark attack.

Many people who have an abnormal dread of sharks, but still cannot resist the lure of the surf, feel they are playing it safe by remaining close to shore. From a logical standpoint, shallow water close to shore would seem almost sharkproof. Statistics, however, do not confirm such thinking, because an examination of a hundred attacks picked at random shows that about 25 percent of the attacks have occurred in water that is no more than waist-deep.

Attempting to find a logical answer to this requires the careful analysis of several considerations. The first may be observed almost any day at the beach. It will be noted that by far the larger number of people are to be found splashing about in water shallow enough to permit them to stand upright if they so desire. Secondly, many sharks frequently cruise in water so shallow that the upper part of their body is exposed with the underside barely skimming the bottom. They do not remain in such shallow water for extended periods, but when searching for rays, crabs, and dead fish being washed ashore, they go where they stand the best chance of finding food.

Then, too, when one takes time to study the contour of the inshore bottom it will be found that only infrequently does the water shoal off from the beach in a level slope. Most often the bottom begins to assume an irregular pattern just beyond the low tide line. At that point, for a considerable distance out, the bottom is a series of hills and valleys with passes in between much like a range of miniature mountains. Fish, sharks included, follow these swash channels and surf fishermen know that more fish may often be caught close to shore than by casting their lure or baited hook out as far as possible.

It is also reasonable to assume that a shark senses the abundance of activity in the shallow water and simply cruises in to see what is causing the confusion. Under normal conditions it will idle along, satisfy its curiosity, and return to deeper water when it reaches the next pass between sandbars. It is not at all unusual for someone in the crowd of surf bathers to cut his foot on a broken bottle or some other sharp object. Before he has time to get back to the beach and have the damage repaired some blood is sure to be spilled. The backwash of the waves will carry the scent out and if there happens to be a shark nearby it is almost certain it will detect it. Such a minor accident certainly does not mean a shark attack is sure to follow, but it cannot be denied that if a shark is close enough to detect even the faintest scent of blood it is going to automatically become more interested than it might otherwise be.

Still another important consideration is that at times almost any shark will strike back if molested. It is quite likely that some attacks result from a person unwittingly kicking a shark. The creature may be moving along nearby, but unseen by the human. A foot kicks out, strikes the shark, and the shark interprets it as an attack by this stranger in its watery world. The blow will not hurt the shark, but if it is in an aggressive mood it may strike back. The result would be a gush of blood and panic on the part of the human. Such a combination could easily contribute to a second and decidedly more serious attack.

For many years fishermen and divers viewed the nurse shark, *Ginglymostoma cirratum,* found north and south of the equator and well into temperate waters on both sides of the western hemisphere, as completely harmless. That they would molest a human was as unthinkable as a rabbit rushing out of the brush and biting a farmer.

They frequent shallow water and because of their extensive range, they are often found where people are swimming. The mouth and teeth are small in comparison to the more rapacious species, but not so small as to preclude a serious bite. They are slow-moving bottom feeders and because of their inoffensive reputation and the fact that it is possible to grab on, some adventurous swimmers will capitalize on such

Nurse shark.

facts and take hold of a nurse shark for a free ride. For the most part these displays of derring-do only bring excited shouts from those who are watching the show. Occasionally, however, the nurse reacts in an unexpected manner and turns on its antagonist. There are numerous records of moderately severe injury from these sharks and it is wise to leave them alone.

Logically, a bolder species can be expected to react in a more vicious manner. Then, too, there are those individuals who will ignore warnings when a shark is sighted and continue swimming. Certainly, most of the time they will get away with it, but they are courting injury and possible disaster. It is always the better part of valor to leave the water until the potential danger is past.

In general terms, physical contact such as grabbing, kicking, or otherwise striking a shark should be avoided. Nevertheless, it should be noted that numerous people credit such tactics with saving their lives. At times a diver or swimmer finds himself confronted with an obviously aggressive shark that gives all indications of intending to make an attack. At such times some have been turned away by being struck with a camera, kicked, or even struck with a fist. Then again, the stage seems to be set so that an attack seems inevitable, only to have the beast demonstrate its unpredictableness by suddenly leaving for no apparent reason.

One classic example was reported to me several years ago by two fishermen whose boat exploded and burned off the lower southwest coast of Florida. Both men had sustained injury during the mishap and one received a deep gash on the calf of a leg. Both were blown overboard by the blast and, of course, there was no time to don lifejackets. The time was about the middle of the afternoon and the only immediately available floating object was a ragged section of the cabin roof.

In desperation they swam for this, but quickly discovered it was not sufficiently buoyant to support even one man. Their only hope was to cling to this piece of flotsam and try to propel it toward a small coastal island they could see in the distance. The man with the bleeding leg removed his shoelaces and fashioned a crude form of a tourniquet which served to staunch the flow of blood to some extent. The wound was deep and both knew that enough blood had been spilled to attract any shark that might be in the vicinity.

They had been kicking and paddling for about an hour when, as they had feared, a shark appeared. It was a hammerhead at least ten feet long and they watched in dread as it began circling, drawing closer each time it went around. The man with the injured leg had lost both of his shoes after he had removed the laces. The hammerhead continued its ominous reconnoitering for several minutes. It was plainly visible in the clear water and the men saw it suddenly turn abruptly and make a swift charge straight toward them. It

Nurse shark.

passed directly beneath the raft, slamming against both men as it swept by.

For several more terrifying minutes the shark continued to circle and the men knew that if it should make even an exploratory bite, the chances of maintaining a grip on the raft would be slight. Twice more the hammerhead rushed toward them, only to veer away at the crucial second. It was as if the creature might have been deliberately tormenting them with its circling and sudden rushes. Then, just as the men had almost resigned themselves to what seemed to be an inevitable fate, the shark casually turned and cruised off to the south.

Even with a favorable current and an onshore breeze, it was nearly midnight before they reached the island, which they had lost sight of after sundown. They were adrift for nearly nine hours and every time they heard a mullet jump or

173

saw a luminescent streak through the black water they were certain the hammerhead, or some other shark, was closing in on them. Except for their dangling feet and legs having been bumped when the shark made his first charge, they had no physical contact with that or any other shark throughout the nine hours.

A similar, yet decidedly more tragic, event occurred in the Gulf on July 2, 1974, about thirty-five miles southeast of the town of Carabelle, Florida. The Edward Horne family of Houston, Texas, was aboard their forty-three-foot cabin cruiser bound for a vacation in the Bahamas. Just before midnight they encountered a small, but severe squall that caused their boat to break up. The Horne couple was able to transmit a Mayday signal several times before the boat sank.

The radio distress signal was heard by the coast guard station in St. Petersburg approximately one hundred and fifty miles southeast. Search and rescue planes were dispatched immediately and, although flares were used, the boat wreckage was not found until near midday. The pilot quickly spotted the Hornes and radioed, "Sharks appear to be feeding." Unable to land on the water, the pilot attracted the attention of a small pleasure craft nearby and directed it to the shipwrecked family, all of whom were clinging to a single life ring.

A coast guard helicopter and the coast guard cutter *Lobos* aided in the eventual rescue, but before the first boat could reach them, the Horne's ten-year-old son, Billy, had been fatally mangled by sharks that cut off an arm and leg. A second child, Edward, died of exposure during the ordeal. All were airlifted to the nearby hospital at Tyndall Air Force Base.

Several members of the family had injured their feet kicking at the attacking sharks. Mrs. Horne reported that at one point while they were in the water a shark became tangled in a line onto which she was holding and began pulling her under. She was able to push herself back to the surface by shoving against the shark's back with her feet. The air force and coast guard airmen stated that the family was ringed by sharks that would have measured at least twelve feet in length. They also reported sighting other sharks cruising about in the immediate area. Considering the apparent aggressiveness of the shark pack, it is likely all members of the family would have been killed had rescue been delayed much longer.

At times a shark will seemingly single out one individual and press the attack relentlessly, even though it actually has to fight other people to continue after its intended victim. The fatal attack on seventeen-year-old Barry Wilson is an example of such an attack.

Wilson and several companions were swimming and skin diving in Monterey Bay off the coast of California on December 7, 1952. Suddenly, his friend, Brookner Brady, saw him seemingly rise up in the water to the level of his thighs. He quickly suspected Wilson was being attacked by a shark and summoned for help from four members of the Sea Otters' Skin Divers Club who were nearby. Putting their own safety in jeopardy, the five young men went to the rescue.

Even though he was surrounded and being helped by the other five, Wilson was struck and gashed time after time by the lone shark. The attack had begun just beyond the breaker line of the surf and as they moved shoreward with Wilson on an inflated rubber float, the water was red with blood flowing from Wilson's numerous wounds. The shark repeatedly shoved and pushed at the five rescuers in its effort to wrest Wilson from them. The creature had ample opportunity to have bitten and possibly killed any of the others, but left them alone except for knocking them aside time after time. In a display of outstanding heroism the five stuck to their task and eventually managed to drag Wilson ashore. Their valiant efforts were in vain because the victim was dead from severe bites and loss of blood.

Considering the bloody water and the obvious feeding frenzy of the shark, it is difficult to find a logical reason as to why it did not turn its attention to one of those attempting the rescue. There are similar cases on record, but occasionally some of the rescuers have been injured in such a long and trying swim. The unidentified shark did not cease fighting for possession of its original victim until the others had carried Wilson out of the water. Only then did the shark turn and swim back out toward open water.

It is well known that underwater explosions will kill, or severely disable many types of fish. Sharks not only resist injury but often such detonations actually attract them. My first chance to observe this came when I was flying with the United States Navy. We made frequent flights to the Pacific islands of Wake and Midway when work was underway to improve the harbors. About once each day the construction crews would set off large charges of explosives to shatter obstructions from the bottom so the debris could be removed with dredges and draglines.

Even before the foam on the surface had settled the area would be littered with dead and dying fish. For the sharks, however, it would be as if the dinner bell had rung. They could be seen cruising about feeding on the abundance of fish. Not only were there sharks in the harbor at the time of the blasting, but in a matter of only a few minutes, numerous ones from the open sea could be seen hurrying through the pass to take advantage of the free feast. Logically, any that were directly over or immediately adjacent to the explosions were quite likely killed, but lacking the previously mentioned swim bladders, they were not sent belly-up to the surface like so many of the fish.

Those of us who were present and interested in the subject pondered the obvious attraction at length. We reasoned that perhaps during the months that the work on the harbors had been in progress the sharks that consistently inhabited the waters around these two islands had learned that explosions meant an abundance of food was to be had. This theory had to be abandoned later, because as we moved to distant islands where no construction work had been in progress, the first explosions invariably drew numbers of sharks without delay. Their almost immediate arrival precluded the possibility that the smell could have drifted seaward.

Rational thinking makes it too farfetched to assume sharks across the vast reaches of the ocean would attach any significance to man-made blasts. When it is considered, however, that many islands owe their existence to countless volcanic eruptions, it is possible that sharks have, over millions of years, become conditioned to associate any violent shock wave with dead and disabled fish that are certain to be present.

Then, too, it is possible that their innate curiosity causes them to investigate anything unusual that occurs within their range. Extensive tests and experiments have been conducted in recent years to determine how far away and by what means a shark can detect an unusual disturbance in the water. It is known that they have reasonably acute hearing and there is still another means known as pressure sensors imbedded in their anatomy known as the lateral lines. This sensory system circles and crisscrosses the head section and extends along both sides for the entire length of the body.

This second "hearing" system is imbedded within the shark's flesh and can best be described as fluid-filled tubes with impulse nerves extending outward toward the surface of the skin. It is believed that the shark depends on this system to detect and be led to any low frequency disturbance in the water. It also appears that if the disturbance is erratic—as opposed to the normal impulse waves emitted by a creature swimming in a normal fashion—the shark's appetite is automatically stimulated. Such a condition might be caused by a large fish that is fighting a hook, or one that has become disabled for some other reason.

Big game fishermen have long known that it is not only whether they are capable of subduing the catch but whether it can be brought to gaff before a cruising shark comes to investigate. Many large fish that would, under normal conditions, easily be able to avoid a shark, are virtually helpless when battling heavy tackle. Trawler fishermen and those employing the use of any net that surrounds schools of fish are often confronted with shark problems. The trapped fish become panicky and the shark senses it.

This sensory system is known to attract a shark's attention when it is far beyond the range of normal hearing and far beyond that of visual contact. Research scientists working on a dependable shark repellent have reasoned that if certain

Speargun pointed at shark.

sounds and vibrations attract sharks, surely there must be others that would frighten them. So far such experiments have met with no success.

Skin divers who hunt reefs and rock piles with conventional spears and spear guns would do well to think twice before taking aim on any shark of four feet or longer. True, it has been done with no adverse effects on the underseas hunter, but he should not lose sight of the previously mentioned fact that a shark is not easily killed. Much depends on the temperament of the individual shark, and this is not to be misinterpreted as the species of shark. Generally, the hunter may experience no difficulty beyond that of hauling his prize to the surface.

On occasions, however, the situation suddenly reverses itself and the hunter becomes the hunted. The fact that the shark has a spear deeply imbedded in its flesh will not impair its ability to inflict serious injury.

Surface fishermen lead the list of people who are injured by sharks. All too frequently an angler will be lulled into a sense of false security because the shark he has caught failed to put up the expected fight. He may even allow himself to be drawn up beside the boat with little more resistance than would be experienced if the fisherman had fouled his hook on a submerged timber. It may be that the angler would like to return to port and be photographed with his catch. To avoid losing his shark he may strike it with a flying gaff and tighten the line to the side of the boat. If the craft is of sufficient size and there is help and proper equipment available, it may be hauled aboard.

In keeping with their unpredictable nature, a shark may not only have refused to fight but may even submit to such drastic treatment as this without much of a struggle. Again, at any given moment, it may become as much of a menace as a newly captured tiger. To have a ten-foot shark suddenly go berserk in the cockpit of a cabin boat is a terrifying experience. Such may happen in the first few minutes, or it may remain passive for a much longer period of time.

On one trip I caught a nine-foot dusky shark, *Carcharhinus obscurus*, and with two helpers aboard, managed to get a line around its tail. We then hauled it up so that it was secured in an inverted position on a heavy gin pole at the stern of the cockpit. I quickly noticed that it appeared to be gravid and I was particularly interested in taking her back to the dock so that I might remove the young for study. I thought we had taken all necessary precautions to prevent trouble by shooting the shark in the head several times with a 30-30 rifle before getting the tail rope in place.

It was a cloudless day and the dusky hung motionless for fully an hour and gave all indications of being dead. As an added precaution, however, I followed a practice I began long ago and wedged a two-foot length of 2 x 4 in the corner of the mouth at the jaw hinge. Almost exactly one hour after the shark had been hoisted from the water, she began to jackknife her body and thrash with such fury that the manila used for the tail rope parted as if it had been no stronger than a cotton clothesline.

In an instant the shark was plunging about in the cockpit, making shambles of deck chairs and other loose items, breaking in the side of a built-in ice chest and crushing the piece of timber wedged in her jaws. To add to the confusion she delivered a total of eleven fully developed and very much alive young sharks. It was not until we had clubbed her head repeatedly with a baseball bat that the furious activity was halted.

When it was safe I gathered up the young and tossed them in the broken ice chest. Then, acting with exaggerated caution, we hoisted the dead shark over the gunwale. After the excitement had subsided and order was restored, I decided to examine one of the young that, by then, had been lying on a bed of crushed ice for about twenty minutes. I was standing by the gunwale and attempting to measure it around the girth, the length having been already' recorded at nineteen inches. Suddenly, this little fellow became so active that it flounced out of my hands. It landed in the water, swam erratically in a circle for a few seconds, and then, seeming to get its bearings, darted away in apparent good health.

Shark hunting from small inshore-type boats is becoming an increasingly popular sport. With the mobility of the boat, the angler has a distinct advantage over the one who is confined to the beach or pier. If the fisherman follows a few common sense rules he can have the sport of catching a large sea creature at a fraction of the cost of his bluewater counterpart who goes far out for marlin, tuna, and other gladiators of the deep.

The sport, however, is not without potential danger, especially if the angler lacks sufficient experience or sure knowl-

Shark at surface grabbing for food.

edge of what a shark is capable of doing. If medium-heavy tackle is used the fisherman's chances are good that an occasional shark may be quickly subdued, or seemingly so. As previously mentioned, large sharks can do extensive damage to a boat and the smaller the boat, the greater the possibility of serious damage. Unlike many large game fish that are almost always caught well offshore, it is not in the least uncommon to catch a seven-hundred- or eight-hundred-pound shark very close to shore.

Just while the triumphant angler is viewing his catch with pride he may suddenly wish he had confined his shark fishing to the relative safety of a well-constructed pier. Frequently, a shark that appears to have been whipped down will erupt in a frenzy and attack the boat and even grab the lower housing of a large outboard engine, making a strong bid to rip it loose from the transom.

Never, under any circumstances, should the fisherman tie a large shark to the boat in a manner that might preclude cutting it free at a moment's notice if trouble begins. If it is to be returned to shore, the only safe way is to get a tail rope on it and start the engine without delay, still being positive there is a sharp knife immediately available to cut it free should the need arise. If the engine is strong enough and the shark can be towed by the tail it will tend to lull it, because the reverse flow of water will deprive it of needed oxygen.

There are times when a shark will attack a boat, even when it is not tethered to it. Some years ago I was casting for bonefish in Florida Bay and I had an encounter with a tiger shark that was longer than my twelve-foot skiff. It cut off what I thought might be a record bonefish and, without considering the possible consequence, I rebaited my light tackle with a strong leader and a much larger hook. I could see the shark still cruising about in the shallow water and I cast toward him. It took the bait almost immediately, but wasted little time in breaking free, but not until it had attacked my boat with such force as to send me sprawling on the bottom boards.

Even though it was free to swim away—something I sincerely wished it would do—it continued to attack the boat. Although it was not restrained in any way, it came perilously close to upsetting the boat and succeeded in ripping off part of the plywood and hitting the freeboard with such force as to crack the gunwale and also start a leak. I managed to get the outboard started quickly and departed posthaste.

When I returned to the marina I had an opportunity to examine the damage and even collect several of its teeth it had left imbedded in the wood. These served to further establish its identification. If it had been tied to the side when it decided to give vent to its rage, there is no question that it would have demolished the boat. I suspect my own chances of survival would have been quite slim if I had found myself in the water with it.

One of the most outstanding examples of someone failing to observe the oft-repeated maxim of "Never trust a dead shark" involved a California surf fisherman. Under normal conditions it would seem that fishing from the beach would be the safest method of capturing a shark. The following incident proved an exception to the rule, but the fault lay in carelessness.

The angler was using heavy tackle and he hooked and fought a ten-foot white shark in a battle that lasted for two hours. When he had the shark in shallow water, he struck it with a short-handled gaff and dragged it ashore by brute force. The shark lay still with its jaws agape and gave all indications of dying.

Aware that sharks can be deceptive, the angler decided to play it safe and wait long enough to be sure. It was late afternoon and after propping his tackle against a rock he returned to his car. He took his time about eating a couple of sandwiches and listened to the evening news on his car radio.

When well over half an hour had passed he returned to the beach and found his shark had not moved; even the mouth was still open. The hook was in full view and the angler foolishly reached inside the mouth to twist it free. As it turned out, it was probably the most expensive hook that fisherman had ever bought. The instant he began to twist it free the shark slapped his jaws shut, locking the man's hand as tightly as if he had caught it in a bear trap.

For the next fifteen minutes the man and shark rolled and tumbled about on the sand. The captive fisherman beat the shark with his free hand and even attempted to gouge out its eyes. Blood was flowing from the man's wrist and arm and if the struggle had lasted much longer the man probably would have died from shock or loss of blood. Eventually the shark opened its jaws and the badly injured fisherman scrambled away.

Keeping his wits about him, he managed to drive to the nearest medical assistance. After a blood transfusion and numerous stitches, he made a successful recovery. He still fishes for sharks, but when one is caught he cuts the stainless wire leader with a pair of wire cutters and lets the *dead* shark keep the hook. In discussing the episode later he said that he was convinced that if the shark had been fully alive it would have cut his hand off above the wrist. He recalled that, although the pain was intense, at no time did the shark increase the pressure. It had simply closed its jaws and kept them closed while it thrashed about.

There are many cases of shark attack that have been witnessed at close range by companions of the victim. In documented accounts, however, there are few times when a person has seen another literally swallowed by a shark, with the observer only a few feet away. Such an event occurred on June 14, 1959, off Alligator Head, La Jolla, California. It was Sunday afternoon and two men, Gerald Lehrer and Robert L. Pamperin, were wearing face masks and flippers. They swam out to a cluster of rocks about a hundred yards from shore to look for abalones, the shellfish that adhere to the side of submerged rocks and are highly esteemed for their epicurean food value.

Reaching what they hoped would be a productive area, Lehrer and Pamperin began making surface dives to examine the rocks. They were separated by only a short distance and as Lehrer surfaced after a dive he glanced toward his companion. He immediately saw the dorsal fin of a shark moving straight toward Pamperin. Shouting a warning to his friend and to other swimmers in the cove, he began swimming toward Pamperin to be on hand if the approaching shark should make an attack and his assistance be needed.

Seconds later he saw Pamperin's body rise high in the water. He realized immediately by the way Pamperin was flailing his arms that the shark had struck him from below. In the next instant, just before he was able to reach the spot, he saw his companion drawn beneath the surface. Still hoping he might be able to help, he arched over in a dive right where Pamperin had disappeared. There was no doubt that the shark had made an attack, but what he saw was something for which he was totally unprepared.

In horror, he stared down at the shark, which he estimated to be about twenty feet long. It was in the process of swallowing his friend. Through a growing cloud of blood, he could see Pamperin's head and arms protruding from the shark's mouth and noticed that the man's face mask was missing and his eyes were looking upward.

As the shark began to move away Lehrer realized there was no possibility of helping the man that only minutes earlier had been his companion on a pleasant outing.

Word of the fatal attack spread rapidly and an intensive search, that included lifeguards in boats, scuba divers, and a coast guard helicopter, was begun. The group continued the search until darkness closed in, but no trace of the victim or the shark could be found. Presumably, the shark was successful in its gristly chore and, having had its fill, swam back out to open water.

Experts who interrogated Lehrer in detail eventually concluded it was a tiger shark, but it had to be largely a matter of guesswork, drawn from a man who had witnessed the tragedy that was over and done with in a matter of only a few minutes from the time the fin was first sighted until the shark swam away.

Similar in nature, but sufficiently different, was a discovery off the Mexican coast near Tampico. In the early days of April

1946, a crew of fishermen were returning to port about two hours before sundown. Nearing the beach they spotted what they first believed to be a small whale that had become stranded on a sandbar. Curious, they changed course to investigate and quickly realized the creature was a large white shark. They might have moved on had they not noticed the lower part of two human legs protruding from the shark's mouth.

There was no movement of the legs to suggest the victim was still alive and the fishermen tail-roped the shark and towed it back to Tampico. In the presence of a coroner, the shark was opened and the body of a young man about seventeen years old was removed. Except for teeth marks, there was no evidence of foul play. Since the man was fully clothed it was assumed that he had fallen from a ship. It was concluded that the width of the man's shoulders had been sufficiently wide enough to lodge in the shark's gullet.

It can only be guessed that the victim's shoulders became wedged in such a manner as to prevent the shark from continuing to swallow. Some freak condition must have also prevented the shark from expelling the body. In such a predicament, its jaw action was probably impaired and as it began to suffocate it may have accidentally grounded itself on the sandbar.

Sea disasters unquestionably account for the largest number of people killed by sharks. The sinking by Japanese torpedoes of the U.S.S. *Indianapolis,* at one minute after midnight of July 30, 1945, undoubtedly set a navy record of horror for men versus sharks. With nearly twelve hundred officers and men aboard, the ship had left the Pacific island of Tinian and was bound for Leyte. After the torpedoes struck and the ship had gone down there were at least nine hundred survivors in the water and most of them were solely dependent upon lifejackets to keep them afloat.

Sharks began to arrive in numbers by sundown of the first day. Throughout the night there could be heard the frantic screams from first one man and then another as they were dragged under by the sharks. In the five days the crew was in the water many died of thirst or injury but, ever present, were the patrolling bands of sharks. When rescue finally arrived only three hundred and seventeen men were still alive. Because of the length of time they were in the water and the fact that they were scattered over such a wide area, there could be no accurate way of even guessing what percentage were shark victims.

When the S.S. *Nova Scotia* went down on November 28, 1942, in the Indian Ocean off South Africa, it probably set a record that hopefully will never be broken. Authorities estimated that about one thousand people who went into the sea alive were taken by sharks.

The reproduction of most true fish is largely a hit-or-miss proposition. The female casts an abundance of eggs and the male releases his sperm in the same area. From that point on the fish leave it to chance for the fertilization of the tiny eggs.

Shark copulation is entirely different, with both sexes joining at mating time. The male shark is readily distinguishable by a pair of copulatory organs called claspers. These finger-shaped organs are located on the inner edges of the two pelvic fins. These are inserted into the oviduct of the female and the sperm is thus introduced. There is no specified length of time for the two to remain together, ranging anywhere from several minutes to a much longer period of time. On occasions the male shark will grasp one of the female's pectoral fins with his jaws and hang on as they swim in an unhurried fashion.

In many species the embryo develops fully within the female, while in others eggs are deposited. There is no maternal care, except as nature decreed it. The oviparous female lays her eggs in reasonably shallow water where the bottom is composed of soft mud. From that point on, the hatching process is a matter of water temperature and time. There is no such thing as a nest, and when the eggs do hatch the mother shark may be in far distant waters.

With viviparous species the female moves into an area of floating seaweed or tangled bottom growth when the young are due to be born. The young thus have some form of shelter

Shark giving birth.

and a better chance of finding food. It has been observed that the female's desire for food diminishes at this period. However, some females have been known to deliver a youngster and immediately turn and swallow it as if it were just another fish. This probably is an abnormal occurrence, but the youngster wastes no time in escaping the moment it is born. It enters the watery world fully equipped, with a full set of teeth, and there is no hesitation in swimming and making a quick grab for the nearest crab or unwary fish.

The flesh of sharks is often used as human food and, in the case of many species, the taste is much the same as fish that are rated as good tablefare. Many people find it to be quite tasty, while others shudder at the thought of eating shark. They often unwittingly do so, however, when it is marketed under different names such as grayfish or whitefish.

Soup made from dried shark fins has long been considered one of the seafood delicacies in many parts of the world. There is a decided art to its proper preparation that originated in the Orient. For perfection, the fins must be from certain species of sharks, while others would have little or no value.

Skin divers, hunting the reefs and rock piles with spears, frequently place themselves in a potentially dangerous position by actually attracting sharks. This is especially true of those using scuba gear which enables them to capture more than one fish before returning it to the boat. A common practice is to attach a captured fish to a clip on the belt. At this point the shark is not only attracted by the erratic sound waves produced by the struggling fish, but there is also the

Removal of live baby shark from left womb cavity of female shark.

faint scent of blood and if the shark is nearby it will see the dangling fish.

If it senses competition from other nearby sharks it may make a quick rush to get there first, occasionally slashing the skin diver as it makes a grab for the fish. Since it has already been established that shallow water is no determent to many sharks, the wading fisherman should also exercise caution for the same reason.

Anglers with a knowledge of the unpredictable habits of sharks frequently tow some form of flotation device and when a fish is caught it is either placed in, or attached to the float. If a shark appears on the scene there is always the possibility that it is in an aggressive mood. In many cases it may only be inquisitive, but there is no way to be sure. At such times the fisherman or skin diver would do well to put a safe distance between himself and any fish he has caught. If the shark wants what it considers a free meal badly enough it is going to take it one way or the other. To be close by while it is doing the taking is risky business.

Two species of fish are frequently found in the company of large sharks. The pilot fish, *Naucrates ductor,* is a trim jack, banded with broad black and silver stripes that encircle the body. They are fast and agile fish and at times as many as several dozen will be seen proceeding, swimming alongside or trailing just behind the shark. A popular belief is that they lead a shark to food. In reality, they accompany the shark only to vie for any scraps the shark may miss while feeding.

The other companion fish is the remora, *Echeneis naucrates*, sometimes called shark suckers. They have a powerful sucker disk on the top of the head which they use to adhere to the shark's skin, generally close to the head and mouth. They, like the pilot fish, are aware that sooner or later they will have an opportunity to dine on leftovers. No friendship exists between the shark and these two and if either should become careless the shark would eat them as quickly as any other fish.

The pilot fish depends on its speed and the remora attaches itself so firmly that it will not be swept off, no matter how fast the shark swims. Both will often be found in the

Shark (sand tiger) with remoras attached.

company of other large fish, hitchhiking and keeping company for the same reason.

In the years I have been observing sharks and their behavior, I have had several encounters which at the time I considered dangerous situations. Most of my near mishaps have been the result of carelessness in handling sharks that have been hooked. It is questionable as to whether the attack on my skiff in Florida Bay—mentioned earlier—would be considered a provoked or unprovoked attack. I am convinced my narrowest escape from a completely unprovoked attack occurred while I was with the navy, stationed at what was then known as the Kaneohe Naval Air Station on the island of Oahu, Hawaii.

Once, while on the island of Maui, three of us bought a thirty-foot, native-built outrigger sailing canoe and decided to sail it back to home base. The trip was interesting, but relatively uneventful until we were off the northeast coast approaching the pass that led into Kaneohe Bay. While we were on this final leg of the voyage two blue sharks, *Prionace glauca,* each about twenty feet in length, began pacing our canoe. At times they cruised so close that first one and then the other would bump against the outrigger.

Having such large sharks so near was somewhat unnerving, but we assumed they would veer off to sea when we turned to cross the reef at the bay's entrance. There was a fairly heavy sea running and the reef was crested with white foam. As we made the turn our lack of experience in sailing an outrigger caused us to capsize.

My two companions held onto the canoe as it was swept over the boiling reef and made the crossing with nothing more than a thorough dunking. As soon as I bobbed to the surface I realized I was in the heavy swells on the seaward side, but very close to the narrow pass. Fearful of being cut and scraped if I tried to swim across the reef, I elected to remain in deep water and swim to the sandy point. I had hardly begun when I spotted one of the two sharks. It was off to one side and several feet below.

Immediately, it began a game of cat-and-mouse with me— sweeping ahead, turning, and coming back. On one of its passes it was so near that my hand brushed against its rough hide. I determined I would maintain a steady but unhurried swimming pace, although it was a temptation to begin thrashing the water in the hope of frightening it away. Growing tired of swimming, I began treading water and I was watching when it began what I was convinced was going to be an attack. In desperation, I drew my legs up and when it was planing up toward me I kicked down with all my strength, delivering a solid blow on the top of its pointed snout.

It caused the shark to turn slightly, but kicking a twenty-foot shark could not possibly have hurt it. My choice was then to either continue my swim in open water for the beach, or take my chances with the sharp coral. I chose the latter, hoping the shark would not risk a possible stranding.

As it developed, my reasoning prevented what seemed to have all of the aspects of a fatal attack. With the aid of a large wave that came just at the proper time, I was lifted and swept over the barrier without a scratch. Reaching the calm water of the bay I reached the beach with no difficulty. As I looked back toward the seaward side I saw a fin cleave the surface several times; the shark was probably still searching for me.

During the encounter my two friends, oblivious as to what was happening on my side of the reef, had managed to right the canoe, minus the mast, and were paddling toward me. Even after they had beached the canoe and I was relating my experience we saw the shark—or maybe first one and then the other—still patrolling the waves on the far side of the reef.

When a swimmer has a close call with a shark it can hardly be classed as an attack until teeth tear flesh. In that particular event I personally considered it at least a form of attack, since I had two physical contacts with the big blue. It is my conviction that it had me at its disposal and was only taking its time. I feel that it was outwitted only when I abandoned the open water in favor of the treacherous waters of the reef.

There are two factors concerning this episode that are worthy of consideration when shark attack is the topic of conversation. Had, for example, the shark swallowed me—and it was certainly large enough to have done so—my demise would have logically been listed as drowning, since there would have been no witnesses. My companions might have reported that we had been accompanied by the two sharks, but this could have been added only as a footnote to the report. It does, however, add credence to the observation of the California lifeguard's conviction that half of the unrecovered drowning victims are the work of sharks.

The second interesting point to ponder is whether or not I acted wisely by kicking the shark. I feel that it served the purpose of startling the predator long enough to enable me to swim into the churning water of the reef. If there had been no alternate route, the blow might only have aggravated its obvious aggressiveness.

I am firmly convinced that when a shark is only exhibiting curiosity it should not be molested. No blow that could be administered by a human could hurt the shark, but it might possibly cause it to withdraw temporarily. I certainly do not

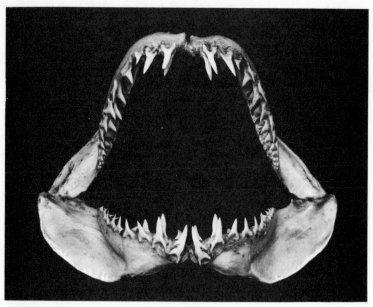

Mako shark jaws.

know for sure and I doubt that anyone else does. After careful consideration over the years I believe if I were ever again in a similar situation I would react in the same manner.

Sharks will continue to occasionally injure or kill humans but, by and large, their danger is grossly overrated. It is unrealistic for *any* resort area along *any* coast to claim its waters are free of sharks. These dangerous creatures of the sea do not respect any boundaries, and if they suspect there is a supply of natural food, such as rays and fish, they are going to investigate from time to time.

Between each shark attack, however, there are going to be many people who are struck by lightning and an even larger number who drown. To set down a list of rules that will safeguard the swimmer is simply impossible. If for no other reason, this is so because of the shark's unpredictable behavior.

From a common sense standpoint it is a wise idea to get out of the water whenever a shark is sighted. Swimming at night or in roiled water is not advisable for the simple reason that it is much more difficult to see a shark that may be becoming more attentive. For reasons previously discussed, it is unwise to remain near a herd of feeding porpoise. There is nothing to be gained by swimming far from shore and if a shark should attack, or show signs of doing so, the swimmer's chances of reaching the beach are lessened.

The most often repeated admonishment is that a swimmer should not exhibit fear when threatened by a shark. Admittedly, this is like the medicine that is easier to prescribe than swallow. No one can be expected to completely sublimate a feeling of apprehension if he feels his life is suddenly endangered. There is, however, unquestionable logic in avoiding the temptation of giving way to panic and flailing the water in a frantic manner. It will certainly do more to attract the shark's attention and suggest that it has come upon a wounded creature. Also, of equal importance, such action reduces the speed of steady swimming necessary to reach the safety of boat or beach.

Wearing bright clothing and any objects such as chrome-plated belt buckles or other glare-reflecting adornments may be quite chic on the beach. In the water they may also attract the attention of a shark. Scuba divers would do well to check their equipment and take precautions to avoid such gear as yellow or white tanks and flippers and shiny regulators.

7

Octopus and Squid

How dangerous is the octopus? Better still, does it pose any threat at all to swimmers, fishermen, and skin divers? If one should undertake a comprehensive study and have at one's disposal all of the literature—scientific, semi-scientific, and supposedly factual reports, not to mention fiction—it would require several years of steady reading. If the study should be extended to include checking, cross-checking, and trying to sift the preposterous from the possible, the investigator might well be at the task for many years.

Should he eventually complete the investigation he would find mountains of evidence to support any of several postulations, whether it be that of no danger, real danger, or any degree of potential hazard that might lie between the two extremes.

The peculiar part about the subject is that the fiction writer, as well as some scientists, are equally guilty of muddying the water by going to considerable efforts to spin a hair-raising yarn, or to debunk any possible threat the octopus might present.

It is generally conceded that when Victor Hugo's widely read novel, *Toilers of the Sea*, was published in 1866, marine scientists and the public at large locked horns in a running dispute that has continued unabated. Hugo was a respected writer and when his hero, Gilliatt, engaged in a life-and-death struggle with a giant octopus, it was so real that the reading public refused to believe such a situation could not possibly have occurred.

When the ominous dread of giant octopuses lurking in their watery caves, just waiting to devour a hapless swimmer, had gained sufficient momentum the "true facts" about the creatures began to flow from several wellsprings. Some were as reliable as possible, others were highly imaginative, while still others were partially informed, and, of course, there were the ubiquitous debunkers whose only stock in store is to pooh-pooh everything. All served to further cloud the issue.

Photography was in its infancy in Hugo's time and suitable equipment seldom, if ever, was available when truly large specimens of octopuses were captured. As a result, the serious student had to depend on sketches—often crudely drawn and inaccurate—to determine if that which had been captured was indeed the same creature as the small octopuses usually available to any marine laboratory.

As the interest waxed, those interested in serious investigation found Hugo had no corner on the market when it came to writing terrifying, and often outlandish, stories about these multiarmed creatures. Centuries before the birth of Christ, Homer wrote in his *Odyssey* of a great monster with many arms. Although the encounter is steeped in mythology, Homer was undoubtedly recounting a legend that was based on the actual sighting of a large octopus.

The same is true of other Greek legends. Many of the early chroniclers and artists were somewhat vague and contradictory as to size, shape, and number of arms. The confusion probably arose when trying to make one and the same creature out of the giant squid and large octopuses, especially since the arms of both animals extend from the head and are similarly equipped with powerful suckers. Aristotle made a more reasonable study of Mediterranean octopuses and described them in his *Historia Animalium.*

Because of the vastness of the seas there is unquestionably still much to be learned about the octopus. As science delves deeper, many new facts will be discovered and established beliefs will be discarded, proven, or altered.

Common octopus.

The basic fact that science agrees upon is that the octopus is of the class Cephalopoda. Close relatives are the squid and cuttlefish. The name cephalopod comes from the Greek word *kephale,* meaning head, and *podos,* meaning foot. Combined and translated into English the words mean "head-footed."

About one hundred fifty species of octopuses have been classified and are found in all of the seas from the frigid waters of the Arctic to the Antarctic, with plentiful distribution in between. Some are barely two inches in length when full grown. The largest is believed to be the Pacific octopus, *Octopus hongkongensis,* with one reliable report of a specimen that had a span of thirty-two feet. The common octopus, *Octopus vulgaris,* is one of the better-known species and is found in most tropical and subtropical seas. When grown, this octopus will have a span of ten feet and weigh nearly fifty pounds.

As the name implies, octopuses have eight arms and in the case of the common octopus, the underside of each of these arms is covered with double rows of suckers. There are normally 240 suckers on each of these arms; thus an individual octopus will have a total of 1,920 sucker disks. The largest of

Octopus with egg cluster—showing sucker disks.

Octopus camouflaged in rocks.

these measures about one and a half inches in diameter and is found near the midpoint of the arm. The suckers gradually diminish in size moving toward the head and the tip of the arm.

These sucker-studded arms serve the octopus as a means of catching and holding food and are employed to some extent as the octopus moves from one spot to another. The web of membrane that spreads from one arm to another near the head is also used when the octopus is moving in an unhurried manner. For a creature that is often referred to with such adjectives as repulsive, grotesque, hideous, and others equally insulting, the gracefulness with which they often move is indeed remarkable. The web undulates in a waving motion and the tips of first one arm and then another lightly touch the bottom as the creature moves. So lithe is this form of locomotion as to give the observer the impression of watching some spectral ballet. This method of swimming is practiced when the octopus is searching for food or simply moving from one hiding place to another.

Generally, the octopus is seen either almost motionless or moving in a seemingly sluggish manner, reaching out with one or two arms and pulling the body and remaining legs along behind. When moving in this manner it appears to be crawling and is in decided contrast to the above mentioned dance.

When it becomes frightened or desires to transport itself from one spot to another in a hurry, its ability to move can come as a surprise to anyone who has not witnessed it. A store of water is maintained within the mantle cavity and in times of stress it is ejected through a funnel or tubelike aperture. This sudden and powerful jet of water will send the octopus away in a rush for a distance of several yards. If more distance is desired, the reservoir is refilled immediately and another jet is expelled. When moving in this manner the eight arms trail behind the fleeing octopus.

But the octopus does not depend on speed alone when its safety is threatened. Inside the mantle cavity is a pear-shaped sac filled with an inky substance of a viscous consistency. As the jet of water is discharged the octopus releases a portion of

Octopus swimming with web extended.

this ink. It was long believed that this cloud ejected behind the octopus served only as a sort of smoke screen, behind which the octopus could hide. More recent investigation has established the belief that the discolored water confuses the predator with both sight and smell.

A moray, shark, or grouper, for example, will spend time striking at the cloud while the octopus is either continuing its escape or has resorted to an almost unbelievable ability to camouflage itself in the vicinity. If necessary, the common octopus can discharge about half a dozen blasts of ink before its supply is temporarily exhausted.

There are two good reasons to believe the discharge of ink is not used as a "smoke screen." Most predators of the octopus depend extensively on their olfactory system to lead them to their prey. Aquarium experiments have led investigators to believe that the ejected ink has a strong octopus smell. Also, it has logically been concluded that the ink cloud would necessarily have to be considerably larger than it normally is to effectively conceal the escaping octopus.

Many sea creatures are remarkable for their ability to change color. Probably the most well known is a boated dolphin. When death approaches a kaleidoscope of changing colors washes over the body. Billfish such as the marlin often seem to glow when in hot pursuit of bait. Flounders and some rays can adjust their chromatophores to match the sea bottom on which they are lying. Few, however, have mastered the art of being able to camouflage themselves in such diversified ways and do it so quickly as the octopus.

The chromatophores of the octopus are so active as to raise some question as to the true color of these creatures. In general terms it is conceded that when completely at ease and not fearful of approaching danger or stimulated by the nearness of food, the most usual color is basically brown. To observe octopuses in a prolonged state of repose, however, is quite difficult because they are constantly alert to the slightest change in their surroundings.

Because of their exceptional eyesight, they can almost invariably spot a diver before he can catch sight of them. If they feel secure in their cave or other hiding place, they will usually hold steady and appear unchanged in color. Prolonged observation, however, will reveal minute color changes. Even a cloud passing overhead will cause them to darken, only to become more their original hue as the sunlight again floods the water.

In moments of excitement, whether it be the approach of a foraging crab or a sudden movement of anything that might represent danger, the color will change quickly. This is especially noticeable if they are sighted moving from one location to another. At times they are capable of blanching to a dull white; then, in a moment, they may display a swiftly changing pattern that ranges from dull red to shades of blue and at times almost as translucent as a jellyfish.

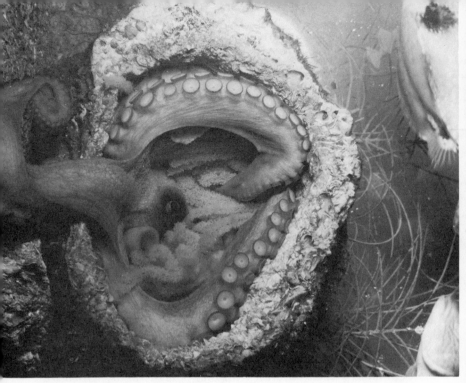

Octopus with egg mass—eye in center.

Frequently they will settle on a section of bottom that may be composed of light brown sand, dull green plant growth, and reddish brown rock or coral. At such times they can cause the arms and mantle to assume a variegated pattern that corresponds to the combination of ground colors. Under such conditions they can seemingly disappear while actually being observed.

The diet of the octopus covers a wide range of food that includes bivalve, fish, lobster, shrimp, crab, and occasionally another octopus. For anyone who has attempted to open the shells of a live oyster, it is a source of wonder as to how an octopus is capable of accomplishing the task. Man must use some prying tool to separate the shells or, under primitive circumstances, resort to smashing the thick shells with a rock. The octopus approaches the task in a more subtle manner. It simply fastens the required number of suckers on both shells of the oyster or any other bivalve and exerts an unhurried but steady pull in opposite directions. This soon wearies the adductor muscles of the bivalve and the shells begin to open and the feast begins.

There have been numerous occasions when vast numbers of small octopuses have invaded extensive clam or oyster beds and virtually wiped out the entire population. Areas where crabs are harvested on a commercial basis have suffered the same fate from time to time.

Because of their extensive range, crabs likely constitute the bulk of octopodan diet. Although it can easily crush the crab's shell with its powerful beak, which it occasionally does, the octopus will at times inject venom into the captured crab and render it helpless. Whether it chooses to crush the carapace and undershell or subdue it with venom, once captured every vestige of the crab's flesh and internal organs is devoured.

At times, when an octopus has taken up residence in a cave that suits it as a semipermanent home, the area around the entrance will be littered with empty crab shells, which frequently are still intact, but if carefully examined it will be discovered that even the jointed legs have been emptied of flesh.

The octopus has numerous enemies, including sharks, large fish, seals, whales, and other types of powerful sea creatures. Quite likely congers and morays are the chief predators of many species of octopus. These serpentine creatures prowl the tunnels, rock piles, and caves where octopuses spend much of their time. The moray's eyesight is feeble compared to that of an octopus, but its sense of smell is highly developed.

Life-and-death struggles between the octopus and moray have been observed, both in aquariums and in their natural habitat. Should, for example, a moray be gliding through a cavern and approach an octopus from the rear, the battle would be over in swift order. The moray would position itself for a strike and its powerful jaws would snap shut on the octopus's head, crushing its victim's brain with its long teeth and swallowing the entire octopus.

If, again, the confrontation occurs in an open area the octopus would bring all of its defensive skills into play. This would include a sudden attempt at escaping by propelling itself away with a jet of water from its funnel and, quite likely, a squirt of ink. If the moray happens to be so skilled as to not be tricked into fruitless attacks at the cloud of discolored water, it would likely continue in pursuit.

The fleeing octopus would attempt the same method for several more times and it might even resort to its ability to camouflage. Unless, however, the moray had been thrown off the trail by the smell of the ink, the camouflage would be of little value because the moray would be able to detect the octopus by scent. If escape were impossible and even if the two animals were equally matched in size and weight, the moray would emerge the victor. But, unless the moray could kill the octopus almost immediately a fierce struggle would ensue.

In an effort to overcome its prey the moray will often grasp one of the arms. Powerful though it is, an octopus is no match for a large moray, but it would not be prevented from engaging in a battle to save its life. With one of its arms locked in the jaws of a moray, the octopus will endeavor to fight off the enemy by enveloping part of the moray's body with as many arms as can be brought into play, and will probably attempt to get in a telling bite with its powerful parrotlike beak. The immediate reaction on the part of the moray (also mentioned in the chapter on the moray) will be that it will immediately form an overhand loop on the tail end of its body and swiftly withdraw the forward portion through the tightly drawn knot. The act is executed so swiftly that the sucker-studded arms are swept off the moray's slime-coated flesh.

The two animals may continue the combat with unrelented fury as the moray bites, twists, bites again, and sweeps the grasping arms of the octopus from its body time after time. If the octopus is skilled enough to keep the moray's jaws away from its head it will likely have to sacrifice a large portion of one of its arms.

It may serve to keep the moray occupied long enough to enable the octopus to make good its escape while its foe is busy eating. The loss of an arm presents only a temporary inconvenience to the octopus. It will, through the process of regeneration, grow a replacement arm. Sharks and fish with powerful jaws are also responsible for amputating one or more octopus arms in a fight.

It is possible for an octopus to cause the death of a human. This statement has often been disputed by competent observers, but there are an equal number who know it to be true. The most controversial question is the danger of venom of an octopus.

Probably the fatality attributed to the bite of an octopus most frequently referred to occurred on September 18, 1954. The victim was a twenty-one-year-old man by the name of Kirke Dyson-Holland. He and a companion, John Baylis, had been spearfishing off East Point about four miles from Darwin, Australia. On their way ashore for a rest the two men scooped up a small blue octopus with a span of only about six inches. Both handled it freely and Dyson-Holland allowed it to slide about over his shoulder. It remained attached to the young man's flesh just below the back of his neck for a moment and then released its grip and dropped back into the surf.

As they reached the beach Dyson-Holland stated that his mouth felt dry and he was experiencing difficulty in swallowing. At this time Baylis noticed a small bleeding wound on Dyson-Holland's back where the octopus had stopped just before it dropped back into the water.

Dyson-Holland began vomiting and was quickly unable to walk. As he was being taken by car to a hospital in Darwin he complained of a pain at the point of the bite. Treatment in the form of adrenalin injection was administered and he was quickly placed in an iron lung. While he remained conscious he said twice: "It was the little octopus." Two hours after the bite he was dead. Since no other cause of death could be found, it was assumed that the octopus was responsible.

In another case, this in Shoalhaven Harbor, New South Wales, another man was wading in the surf and stepped on a small octopus, also reported to be of a bluish color. It bit him on the big toe and according to witnesses, he was dead five minutes later. Admittedly, this second account leaves room for doubt, especially since no dates or names were reported. Also, a period of only five minutes seems an exceedingly brief time for any known venom to move from the toe to a point of the body that would cause death.

There are numerous accounts of people suffering varying degrees of ill effects after being bitten by small octopuses. Often the victim hurriedly disposes of the creature and only on rare occasions is the identity of the species recorded.

There is some question as to the exact method by which octopodan venom is injected. Dissection discloses that the poison gland, which is oval in shape, is located in the body just behind the head. The general belief is that the venom is injected by the beak, but the route it follows after leaving the gland and reaching the beak is not clearly understood. The most logical conclusion is that it flows along a shallow groove on the inside edges of the lower mandible and is introduced as the wound is made.

It should be mentioned that while the octopus beak is frequently referred to as "parrotlike," it resembles a parrot's beak in an inverted position. The lower mandible is considerably larger and closes over the upper portion.

The mouth is a complex organ with the beak in the center of the part known as the buccal mass. This is located beneath the mantle on the anterior portion of the head. The radula, which is part of the mouth and, more specifically, the front of the tongue, consists of very small recurved teeth. Its function is to pulverize bits of flesh torn off by the beak and force it down the esophagus.

The second method by which an octopus can kill a human is simply by holding him underwater until death comes by drowning.

It is certain that an octopus of average size does not include any large creature in its diet. Nevertheless, and under certain circumstances, it is possible for an octopus with a span of only six feet or so to trap a grown man.

It is not unusual for an octopus to reach out of the water to capture certain types of semiaquatic crabs that feed in the shallows. There are even credible reports that some species lurk near the shoreline and capture rats that come to feed at the water's edge. While it is highly doubtful that an octopus would intentionally attack a human without provocation, it might grasp a foot or a hand, mistaking it for a crab or small fish. There are numerous records of this having happened, and even cases where they have reached out of the water and grasped a foot of someone moving along over rocks near the shoreline.

Such would have to be termed accidental, or attacks by mistake. Far more serious results stem from provoked attacks when a skin diver injures or attempts to capture an octopus. If there is no route of escape the creature will bring its sucker-studded arms into play with potentially disastrous results for the human hunter.

At this point it is timely to discuss the suckers and how they operate. It has been mentioned that the common octopus, for example, has 240 suckers on each of its eight arms. Considering their relatively small size, each disk has amazing holding power. To form a clear picture of these suckers, one has only to compare them to rubber suction cups frequently used to attach various items to smooth surfaces. If the surface is moist and the suction cup is sufficiently pliable, it is well known how difficult it is to remove it by pulling on it because of the partial vacuum that is formed between the cup and the surface.

Each octopus sucker is much the same, with the holding power depending on the diameter of the disk. The fundamental difference between a rubber suction cup and those on an octopus arm is the creature's ability to hold or release at will. There is a small opening in the center of each disk and the octopus can, through this small hole, increase the pull of the vacuum or release it entirely and take a fresh grip in less than a second. To make this uncanny ability even more complex, the octopus can change the position of part of its arm, while still retaining an unyielding grip with another part of the same arm.

The moray can rid itself of the sucker disks because of the thick coating of slime on the body. Wet human skin affords a much more secure surface. If a skin diver is knowledgeable of octopodan anatomy and if he has some weapon such as a

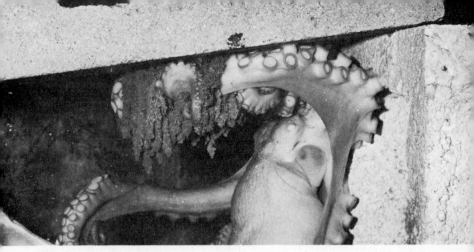
Octopus with egg mass.

knife or spear, he can quickly relieve himself of such an un-
wanted embrace. One need only thrust the sharp-pointed
weapon into the center of the octopus's head squarely between the eyes. If the weapon is twisted about it will destroy
the creature's brain, automatically releasing the suckers.

Hacking away at the individual arms is far less rewarding
for three good reasons. One, the muscles in the octopus arm
are tough and difficult to cut through quickly. Two, the octopus appears indifferent to pain and the loss of even two or
three arms does not seem to concern it. The element of time
is the third reason, and this is of vital importance to the skin
diver who is not wearing scuba. Without a supply of air to
draw from, the length of time he can remain submerged is
indeed brief. This peril was graphically impressed on me
some years ago while on a sailing trip in the Caribbean.

We had anchored our schooner in a sheltered cove and my
companions had gone ashore in the dinghy to explore the
small island. The water beneath the schooner was exceptionally clear and I decided to don my face mask and explore the
bottom. There were endless parades of gay-colored fish passing beside a coral reef. I had taken my knife from its sheath
and was about to cut a particularly desirable sponge loose
from its holdfast when an octopus reached out and took hold
of my left wrist. It startled me and as I felt the suckers grip
my flesh I will admit I was somewhat frightened. My knife

had a finely honed edge and I managed to slice through the grasping arm without much difficulty. Instantly, the suckers released and I grabbed the lifeless appendage.

Quickly returning to the surface, I scrambled ashore and began examining the portion of the octopus arm. One such encounter should have been enough, but for some reason I decided I would like to capture the entire animal. Tossing the rubbery length of flesh aside, I swam across to the ship, climbed up the Jacob's ladder, and located a long metal spear we occasionally used to hunt fish.

Doubtful that I would stand a chance of finding the octopus the second time, I decided I could at least get the sponge I had been about to cut. When I reached the bottom I quickly located the sponge. Nearby was a patch of fernlike bottom grass and there, looking none the worse for its loss, was the octopus. It flowed through the ferns and worked its way into a small hollow near the base of the coral wall. This time it was dull gray in contrast to the mottled brown it had been when I first contacted it.

As I moved closer I could guess it had already spotted me and I had an excellent opportunity to observe the change of color that flushed over its body. When I had watched for a long moment I found that I must again kick off for the surface for a fresh breath of air. To mark the spot, I jabbed my spear into the sandy bottom near the base of the coral wall.

When I returned it had again changed color and so nearly did it match the background that it required several seconds to spot it. The crevice was shallow like a groove along the base of the coral wall. It had positioned itself with its arms extending in either direction. Without wasting precious seconds, I plunged the spear into the bag-shaped body. For a brief moment there was no movement. I wondered if I had killed it, but the thought was barely formed when there was a flurry of action.

As I pulled back on the spear I caught a glimpse of one of its arms as it reached up and grasped the shaft. I saw at least two other arms clutching at the irregular outcroppings of coral. Almost at the same instant, still another arm closed

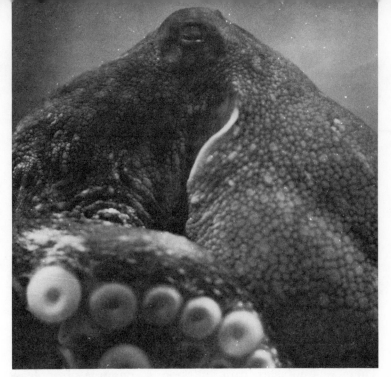

Octopus with eye at top.

around my left ankle. As I attempted to pull free there was a spurt of purple ink that clouded the water around me.

Instinctively I attempted to push the arm from around my left ankle with my right foot. As I did still another arm circled my right leg. For a fleeting moment the entire situation seemed absurd and I found myself thinking of the fable of the tarbaby. The more I struggled, the more involved I became. Releasing my grip on the spear handle, I fought the water and tried to shove myself away from the coral. Only a few pounds can hold a strong swimmer anchored if he must depend on his arms alone to rise to the surface.

As people sometimes do in a moment of mounting tension, I found myself trying to analyze, in a detached manner, the sensation of minor things. In this case I was trying to form an opinion of how the sucker disks felt as they drew at my flesh; almost as if I was performing some laboratory experiment.

Octopus.

There was no sharp pain, but more a sensation of unpleasantly warm points around my ankle and leg.

Again I slipped my knife out of the sheath and leaned over to cut myself free. I was becoming increasingly conscious of the mounting need for a breath of air. Crouching, I attempted to see through the water clouded by the discharge of ink. Suddenly, the tarbaby story was no longer a humorous analogy. Another of the muscular arms had closed around the back of my neck.

At that moment I experienced a moment of near panic. The octopus was holding a firm grip on both the coral and my body. I had been drawn down so that my face was close to the creature's body and just then I saw one of its expressionless eyes. Sweeping my right arm around, I drove the blade of the knife into the flesh near the eye and began twisting it from side to side.

The octopus seemed to shudder and the arms were releasing their grips. I had been down so long that I had to fight off an almost irrepressible temptation to gasp for breath. A new flood of ink obscured my vision, but I realized I was no longer being held prisoner. The vital need for fresh air made my arms and legs feel heavy and lethargic, but I was kicking and stroking for the surface for that coveted breath of air.

After I had rested and was able to reconstruct the two encounters I reached the conclusion that when the octopus first clutched my wrist, it did so believing it was a crab or perhaps a spiny lobster. When I returned and struck it with the spear, it was simply fighting back at the thing that had injured it. How long it would have held me if I had not been able to bring the knife into play is questionable. It is certain that my remaining time to continue the struggle was measured in a very few seconds.

When I dived again I tied a line on the spear handle and hauled the octopus to the surface. Stretching it out on the deck of the schooner it measured a little over seven feet from one arm tip to the other. I could not determine the species, but I suspect it was a fairly large specimen of the common octopus.

In the Puget Sound region in the state of Washington there are several scuba diving clubs that hold periodic contests to capture specimens of the Pacific octopus. Some of those taken are quite large. Those with a span of fifteen feet and weighing well over a hundred pounds are not uncommon.

In his book, *Kingdom of the Octopus* (Sheridan House, 1960), Frank W. Lane reports an account in which a professional diver and underwater cameraman, John D. Craig, had a frightening encounter with an octopus. The episode occurred off the coast of Lower California near San Benito Island. Craig, dressed in helmet and diving suit, had descended into a large rocky hole. He discovered two large octopuses were in the hole with him.

As he began to rise to the surface one of the creatures grabbed him. It was unable to find a secure grip on the loose gravel on which it had been resting, but threw several of its arms around the diver and held on. When he reached the surface Craig's attendants began hacking off the arms with axes. One of these arms was measured and preserved. The portion that was kept was eight feet, two inches and Lane estimated the octopus must have had a span of about eighteen feet.

Because most popular swimming beaches are generally those areas with sandy bottoms, such places are seldom frequented by octopuses because they offer little or no shelter. As a result, the surf bathers will seldom encounter one. The most likely candidates to experience an unpleasant meeting with one of these primitive sea creatures is the skin diver not equipped with a supply of air strapped to his back.

If he has no way of breaking free, it should be remembered that even an excellent swimmer can be restrained by being attached to a weight far lighter than his own body weight. Therefore, serious consideration should be given to the fact that an octopus of modest size can exert a holding power of several hundred pounds if it can grip some solid bottom object.

Squid

Even the most fanciful horror stories concerning the octopus could not compare to the potential danger that is present in the form of the giant squid. If nature had so decreed it, these truly enormous cephalopods could rule the seas, making it unsafe for anyone to venture forth in any craft short of a large and well-armored vessel.

It has been estimated there are over 350 species of squid, ranging in size from the tiny *Sandalops pathopsis,* that measures less than one inch, to the largest, *Architeuthis,* that is known to attain a length of sixty feet. There is substantial evidence to strongly suggest some squid even exceed a hundred feet in length.

The method by which these estimates are made are by reconstructing parts found washed ashore and taken from the stomachs of sperm whales. For an example of how this reconstruction is done, smaller squid of a certain species will have sucker disks of a certain diameter. One that is half again as large will have correspondingly larger disks. When part of one with disks twice as large as the first specimen are compared, it is a matter of simple arithmetic to make a reasonably accurate estimate of size.

While the squid and octopus are both members of the Cephalopoda class and are similar in many respects, they are separated into two distinct orders, with the squid being a decapod because it has ten "feet" as opposed to the eight of the octopus. However, the term decapod can be misleading, because both the octopus and the squid have eight arms. The difference lies in the fact that in addition to the arms, the squid has two tentacles which are much longer than the arms. These tentacles are capable of being retracted and extended.

The squid's tentacles are equipped at the ends with claw-studded suckers which are considerably more destructive than the regular suckers. In the headlong slaughter of the world's whale population, countless numbers of captured specimens have been observed to bear unmistakable circular scars left by the fearsome suckers of squid tentacles.

As has been mentioned, the octopus is by nature a secretive creature that frequents coral reefs and other underwater obstructions that afford places of quick concealment. In contrast, the larger squid prefer the open sea, descending to great depths during the day and rising to the surface at night.

The body of the squid is cigar-shaped with a horizontal fin at the posterior end. This flat fin serves a dual purpose in that it acts as diving plane and rudder when the squid uses its siphon to jet backward. It also is used to propel the creature forward when it wishes to move in that direction.

Of the two, the octopus and squid, the latter is by far the faster and more agile. The siphon or nozzle—like the funnel of the octopus—is positioned on the ventral side and can be directed either forward or aft, enabling swift movement in either direction. The squid can store a larger supply of water in its mantle cavity than can an octopus. Some species are capable of attaining sufficient velocity to jet their bodies well out of the water and sail through the air with such speed as to resemble flying fish.

The head of both octopus and squid are much alike, with the same sharp beak concealed in the buccal mass. While serving the same purpose—that of flesh-rending mandibles—the beak of the squid is decidedly more powerful. Those who have fished for large specimens have reported that even the

Common squid.

strongest wire leaders have been snipped in half with apparent ease.

Proof of the sharpness and crushing power of squid beaks has been well established, but never more graphically than in 1940 when Michael Lerner, renowned international big game fisherman, fished for the Humboldt squid, *Dorsidcus gigas,* off the Peruvian coast.

The Humboldt squid is known to attain a weight of about three hundred pounds and a length, with arms extended, of twelve feet. If the two tentacles were included, the measurement would exceed the above length by several additional feet.

Although well equipped with a large and speedy craft and accompanied by men who had prior experience with these creatures, Lerner and his fellow fishermen were hardly prepared for the power and savagery of their quarry.

Knowing the habits of the squid, they fished at night when vast schools were near the surface. Except for gaining valuable experience, the initial trip was virtually fruitless. They were using heavy rods, strong lines, and terminal tackle that consisted of hooks and wire leaders designed for big game fishing. Setting the hook was no problem, but almost the instant a squid began to fight it discouraged the fishermen in two ways. One was to drench the occupants of the cockpit with powerful jets of water and ink that discolored much of the boat. Then, before they could be gaffed and hauled aboard, they easily snipped the leaders with their beaks and darted away.

Not to be outdone, the Lerner expedition returned to port and revamped their tackle. This time they used clusters of

Common squid.

even larger hooks and steel leaders of greater test. To protect themselves from the jets of ink, they fitted cloth hoods over their heads. Once again, the squid were found in plentiful abundance and, while the increased leader strength was occasionally worthwhile, other squid of unknown size severed even these. On one occasion when the men were attempting to haul a gaffed squid aboard it bit a large chunk out of the tough wooden handle of the gaff.

The savagery with which the squid fought exceeded that of a pack of hunger-crazed sharks. Once they would observe that one of their own members was in trouble, others would rush in and bite chunks of flesh from the one being pulled toward the boat. Men who have engaged in similar fishing expeditions are convinced that if a human should fall overboard with numerous squid nearby he would be ripped asunder in a matter of only a few minutes.

Before Thor Heyerdahl and his crew left Peru to cross the Pacific on the raft *Kon-Tiki* in 1947, knowledgeable marine biologists from numerous places warned them of the potential danger of being attacked by Humboldt squid. The warnings were heeded and during some nights they would observe very large creatures glowing with luminescence just below the surface. From Heyerdahl's description, they could well have been the dreaded monsters, but there were no attacks.

The Humboldt is only one species of large and dangerous squid. They occur at widely separated parts of the world and have occasionally established themselves as killers of men.

There is little doubt that they are also man-eaters, but the latter is only a logical assumption that has never been satisfactorily proven.

There have been reliable reports of squid attacking large and modern ships. The best authenticated attacks have been observed from the bridge and other lofty perches where the action of the squid could be clearly seen. Collisions between ship and squid have also occurred on numerous occasions, but these should not be classed as attacks. However, when a squid is observed to be deliberately overtaking a fast-moving ship and lunging at the side of the hull at a point near midship, it is reasonable to assume it to be an intentional and unprovoked attack. No damage is done, but they do give some idea of the fury of certain squid. The accounts are too numerous to list, but they happen as often today as back in the days of sail.

Accounts of giant squid reach far back into recorded history and the Norwegian kraken is probably the most famous of all. The Protestant Bishop Erik Pontoppidan wrote extensively about this giant squid in his *Natural History of Norway,* the English edition of which was published in 1755. The bishop and other serious chroniclers of the kraken were branded as fakes by many scientists. Many years later entire arms, parts of tentacles, and sections of the massive bodies were brought under study of museum scientists. When more and more parts reached first one laboratory and then another, those people who had been sure the kraken was something out of mythology began to realize there must truly be such a monster.

Skepticism is an important element of the scientific world, and well it is, for scientific facts would be little more than idle prattle and folklore if reasonable proof of a fact were not demanded. There are times, however, when skepticism can be a two-edged sword. Fear of ridicule on the part of conscientious observers often causes them to keep silent when faced with the seemingly unbelievable. By doing so, they frequently withhold valuable information that may be the missing piece of a jigsaw puzzle that is slowly taking shape.

An incident involving a very large squid would quite likely

have evaporated after a few tellings, had it not been for a twelve-year-old boy's determination to prove what had happened by holding onto some physical evidence. The incident occurred on October 26, 1873, near Portugal Cove, Newfoundland. On that day Theophilus Piccot and Daniel Squires went out to net herring. Piccot's son, Tom, was allowed to join the men in the dory so he could begin to learn that art of fishing.

At one point during the day the fishermen observed what at first appeared to be a raft of seaweed. As they drew nearer they realized it was the floating body of some strange sea creature. Intrigued by the obviously slick skin, they prodded it with a boat hook. The act almost cost them their lives. What they had found was a huge squid. Why it was lying almost motionless on the surface, especially in daylight, is a mystery. It might have been injured or it might simply have been acting in an atypical manner.

Whatever the reason, the squid reacted in a violent manner. It began churning the water and lashing out at the dory with arms and tentacles. One of the tentacles snaked over into the boat while one of the thick arms held the small craft fast. At the same time the squid began biting at the gunwale with its beak.

Having frequently heard of the dreaded kraken of Norwegian fjords, the fishermen were certain they were doomed. After fighting back with oars and struggling to keep their dory afloat by almost constant bailing, the men were ready to accept the inevitable. Not so with young Tom Piccot. He grabbed a hatchet and heroically began chopping alternately at the grasping arm and tentacles. His efforts were rewarded when he managed to sever one of the tentacles and then one of the sucker-studded arms. The amputations caused the squid to cease its attack on the boat and the human occupants watched in horrified dismay as it darted about, under and around the boat, emitting great clouds of ink.

Not wishing to further provoke the creature, the two men began to row for shore with all possible haste. Fascinated with the encounter, young Tom Piccot insisted on keeping the sections of the arm and tentacle he had chopped off with his hatchet. Once safely back at Portugal Cove, Squires and the elder Piccot spread the story and were accused of exaggerating or perhaps even fabricating the entire yarn.

Meanwhile, Tom tossed the section of the arm ashore and while he was examining the tentacle, he looked up and saw that several dogs had grabbed the arm and were racing away with it. To vindicate themselves, the two fishermen led some of the townsfolk down to the waterfront to prove their story by confronting them with physical evidence. The boy had managed to safeguard the tentacle which measured nineteen feet and obviously represented only a portion of the entire length. It alone was enough to convince the most skeptical that the strange encounter had indeed happened.

Because it was unlike anything any had seen, it became an object of curiosity and was hurriedly delivered to a Reverend Moses Harvey who was an ardent student of marine life. The Rev. Harvey had frequently been able to identify odd sea creatures brought back by various fishermen. He viewed the portion of the squid tentacle as an exciting find, having some knowledge of the giant kraken. His enthusiasm was beyond bonds when, less than a month later, four other fishermen trapped a giant squid in a seine. In the excitement as they hauled the seine to the beach they chopped the creature's head loose from the body, but managed to get both parts ashore. The Rev. Harvey paid them ten dollars for their catch and had it hauled to his house in a large cart. There he displayed it to countless curious visitors and before it began to spoil he took careful measurements, recording the overall length at thirty-two feet.

For reasons still unexplainable, the decade of the 1870s proved to be a decidedly unusual one as far as large squid were concerned. Throughout that period countless very large specimens were found floating on the surface of the waters off Newfoundland. Some were dead, others were mysteriously disabled, while still others showed no signs of physical injury, but were apparently disoriented. Whatever the reason, the myth of the kraken was proven to be fact; and this after over a century since the English publication of Bishop Erik Pontoppidan's book.

Scientists who had stoutly maintained that no squid ever exceeded a length of several feet were face to face with entire specimens. One of the largest had a mantle fifteen feet long with thirty-six-foot tentacles. Much of the credit should be accorded to Tom Piccot and the Rev. Harvey, since it was through the boy's bravery and curiosity and Rev. Harvey's determined pursuit of the subject that what had long been branded as foolish folklore was quickly converted into scientific fact.

So much investigative work was done by Rev. Harvey that his name was eventually incorporated in the classification of this long-fabled creature. The same squid is today known as *Architeuthis harveyi*. One of the reverend's greatest disappointments came in 1879, when a crew of fishermen captured a living specimen that, according to their report, had an overall length of fifty-five feet with arms as large around as a man's thigh. Not knowing the value of their catch, the creature was killed and hacked to pieces, with much of the flesh being used as fish bait.

The proof of these very large squid has been well established, but scientists are still divided into two camps when the question of whether or not they would make an unprovoked attack on a human swimmer is posed. There can be no denying that large species possess sufficient armament to subdue very large prey. In all fairness to the skeptics, however, it should be kept in mind that many creatures could, by human standards, quickly destroy creatures several times the size of man, yet some of these apparently choose to lead an inoffensive life where people are concerned.

There are so many species of squid that cover such a wide range of size, that both those who are certain of the danger and those who prefer to dismiss the idea could be right. Much depends on the species under study. It is an established fact that the Humboldt squid is responsible for extensive destruction to schools of yellowfin tuna, *Thunnus albacares*, with successful attacks on specimens weighing fifty pounds or more.

As anyone who has fished for these large tuna will testify, they are swift and powerful fish. Experienced anglers know

Squid capturing yellowfin tuna.

that even after an extensive battle with rod and reel, just the act of hauling one aboard can present a problem that is seldom accomplished by a lone angler. They can, and often do, fight savagely even after being brought to gaff. The tuna is only one type of large fish preyed on by large squid, but it is singled out to establish an important point. By comparison, a tuna's speed in swimming far exceeds that of man and its agility in the water is exceptional. If a two-hundred-pound man with the aquatic ability of an Olympic swimmer were to attempt to subdue a tuna one-fourth his size in open water, the man would be cast aside in a matter of seconds. In contrast, a large squid could not only stop a tuna but it could kill and begin to feed on it in minutes.

Since a squid equal in weight to the hypothetical man can grasp, kill, and devour the same tuna, it seems absurd to believe one of these creatures would be fearful of a human adrift in the sea. True, man is not an established part of a squid's diet, but neither is he part of a shark's diet.

The most outstanding and best-documented episode involving an unprovoked attack of squid against man occurred in late March 1941. On the twenty-fifth of that month the troopship *Britannia* was sunk by the German raider, *Santa Cruz*, in the Atlantic about 1,400 miles west of Africa.

One of the *Britannia*'s officers, Lieutenant R. E. G. Cox, and eleven other survivors were clinging onto a raft so small that most had to hold on to the sides, taking turns sitting on the tiny craft. Their ordeal lasted five days before a Spanish ship rescued Cox and two naval officers, all that remained of the original twelve.

According to Cox's report, a large squid grabbed one of the men, clutching him with a tentacle and pulling him below the surface where the man was not seen again. Later, Lt. Cox was attacked by a squid which gripped him around the leg, held on briefly and then let go. The claw-studded suckers

Yellowfin tuna being gaffed.

caused intense pain and the circular scars on Cox's leg were still evident many years later. Some were about an inch in diameter.

Whether the seven unaccounted for seamen fell victim to squid was not known. Some may have been, but it is equally likely they simply sank into the depths as a result of exhaustion. It just so happened that Lt. Cox actually saw one of the men taken by a squid and the deep scars on his own legs were unquestionably those left by a squid.

Some diehard skeptics, determined to dismiss the potential danger of squid, have stated that the flesh of these creatures is too fragile to enable them to represent a threat. This type of argument is, however, only valid in some cases. It is known that certain species of very deep-water squid do have exceedingly fragile flesh. This is a prime example of how some debunkers will distort facts by singling out a few species in an order that boasts about 350 varieties. By using only these and ignoring many others they can present a seemingly valid argument.

Any saltwater fisherman, whether commercial or sportsman, knows that the flesh of many squid is exceptionally tough. They are often used in trolling for large fish because it is known that the creature is tempting to many types of fish, plus the important fact that a strip of squid flesh will, because of its toughness, stay on a hook far longer than would some conventional fish often used as bait.

Despite some of the frightening and occasional fatal encounters with large squid, it may be safely said that they represent little or no threat to the safety of those who go to the beach to swim. The small ones will scurry for safety when a larger creature draws near. The large and potentially dangerous ones prefer to live where they can rise to the surface and descend to great depths at will.

Should, in infrequent cases, one of these big ones be found alive, but out of its natural element, it would be well to leave it alone. As for the shipwrecked sailor or downed airman adrift in open sea, he can only hope and pray that rescue will reach him before he is set upon by any of a number of dangerous sea creatures, including large squid.

8

Rays, Devilfish, Mantas, and Sawfish

There are many types of rays ranging from those smaller than a saucer to giants that measure well over twenty feet from one side to the other and weigh two tons or more. Many are of the suborder Squaloidea and closely related to the shark.

Like sharks, they have cartilaginous skeletons instead of bones found in true fish. It has long been debated whether sharks or rays evolved first. Some claim the shark may be an advanced form of the ray, while other scientists maintain that, while closely related, rays and sharks developed independently.

There are several species of rays that are armed with venomous spines located at the base of the tail or somewhere along the length. For the human fisherman or surf bather it makes little difference as to the specific type. The important fact is that certain species can, and often do, inflict extremely painful and frequently dangerous wounds.

Most stingrays found north of the equator are fundamentally creatures of salt water, well distributed in all tropical and subtropical water. Occasionally, any saltwater stingray will be found foraging along the bottom of rivers in their search for food. In the warm months their natural habitat is the shallow water of bays and near the beach of open ocean. Some species, such as the southern stingray, *Dasyatis*

225

Two southern stingrays gliding over bottom.

americana, are fairly common as far north as the New Jersey coast.

The round stingray, *Urolophus halleri,* of the Pacific is common from the California coast southward. This ray differs primarily from the southern stingray and the Atlantic variety, *Dasyatis sabina,* in the location of the barb on the tail. It is placed farther back toward the tip, thus increasing the chance that it will be driven into a human foot that may accidentally step on the ray.

The largest of the stingrays is the roughtail, *Dasyatis centroura,* with some specimens measuring fourteen feet in

Southern stingray.

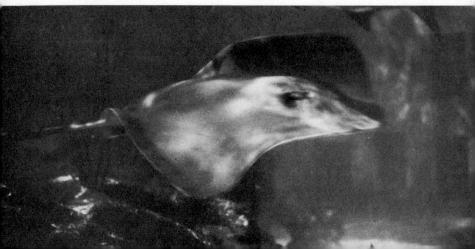

Round (Pacific) stingray.

length and weighing well over three hundred pounds. In the warm months it moves into the shallow bays, retreating to deep water well offshore in the winter. Its range extends from New England southward. Closely related species are found in the Atlantic waters of South America.

The southern stingray is one of the largest and most common of those found in the Atlantic and, while its near relatives differ in size and shape, it exhibits characteristics typical of most stingrays. For this reason it will be discussed in more detail than the others. This species, when fully grown, reaches a width of at least five feet and often exceeds seven feet in length. Those most commonly encountered by swimmers and anglers are usually much smaller. This is true because, as with most sea creatures, there is a greater abundance of younger members than those that manage to survive long enough to reach maturity.

In general appearance stingrays are much the same, although some may be nearly round while other species are somewhat rhomboid in shape. The pectoral fins are greatly enlarged, extending from the head and outward, closing near the tail so that a flattened disk is formed. All are basically bottom dwellers, as opposed to the free-swimming mantas, and find their food in the form of crabs, small fish, clams, other shellfish, and worms. The mouth and gill slits are located on the underside near the head and the teeth are

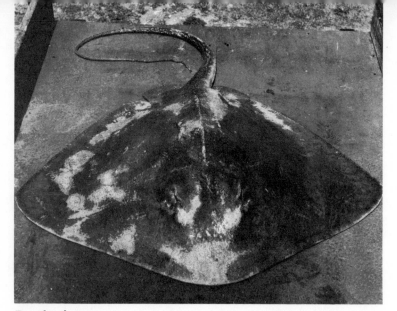

Roughtail stingray.

rounded and designed for crushing shellfish. The teeth are of no consequence as far as the danger of these creatures is concerned.

Unlike the oviparous skates, the young of the stingrays are born alive. When resting they make a practice of settling on the bottom and covering the majority of their flat bodies with mud or sand, so that only the eyes, spiracles, and whiplike tails are left exposed. Thus they are able to see, breathe, and their weapon of defense is ready for instant action.

The tail of the stingrays is quite thick at the base and tapers gradually to a point and is often as long, or longer, than the body. One exception is the round stingray of the Pacific. In this species the tip of the tail is slightly flattened in the form of a small fin. The weapon that makes all stingrays, large or small, dangerous is the spine located on the dorsal side of the tail.

In the southern variety, as with most other species, it is attached to the flesh about a third of the way back along the tail. This spine is a bonelike spear that may measure from one to seven inches in length. It is slightly oval in shape with a decidedly sharp point. Both sides are saw-edged with recurved barbs that make removal difficult once it has been driven into flesh.

The stingray cannot be classed as aggressive in any sense of the word. The dangerous spine is strictly a weapon of defense and is used for no other purpose. Because rays carry a considerable amount of flesh, they quite logically are potential prey of numerous fish. Many species of sharks are their most persistent enemies and, oddly enough, sharks seem undaunted by the venomous spines that would deter many other sea creatures.

This has been well established by the fact that sharks are frequently caught with a dozen or more spines imbedded in the flesh around the mouth. Examination of the stomach contents of sharks has revealed stingray spines, some of which have penetrated the stomach wall and become lodged in the abdominal flesh.

Throughout the year in tropical waters and during the warm months in more northern latitudes the stingray becomes a menace to humans. Warm shallow waters attract these rays, frequently in large numbers. It is here they give birth to their young and prolong their stay to harvest their choice of food.

Because of their habit of concealing the majority of their body beneath a thin covering of silt, they are virtually hidden even in clear water. The result is that surf bathers and fishermen wading the shallows often step on one. At that instant the stingray struggles to free itself and at the same time its tail whips swiftly to discourage what it interprets as an aggressor. Since the tail is not aimed at a specific target in the manner of a striking snake, there is only about a fifty-fifty chance that the spine will be driven into a foot or ankle.

In a matter of one or two seconds the wildly flailing tail may lash the human foot or ankle several times. In this brief moment the human has felt the slick muscular body struggling beneath his foot and, quite logically, withdraws in haste. With luck he will have experienced nothing more serious than a minor fright and, if the water is clear, he will likely see the ray swimming swiftly away, leaving behind a cloud of roiled silt. The natural human reaction is to leave the area with all possible speed. Such a hegira is totally unwarranted since, having made good its escape, the stingray has no intentions of returning to do battle. It will continue swimming until it feels it has put a safe distance between itself and that which molested it. At such a time it will glide back down to a new spot on the bottom and once again fan its wingtips until it has covered its body with sand or mud.

If the venomous spine does make contact with foot or ankle the victim will feel a sharp stab of pain. Here again, the element of chance enters the picture. The spine may have struck a glancing blow. In such a case, the serrated edge will have cut a gash in the human flesh similar to a wound that would result from being slashed with a sharp hacksaw.

While such a victim will almost invariably experience varying degrees of pain and envenomation, he may well count himself lucky to have received a cut as opposed to the victim of a direct puncture. The ray's tail is muscular and swift in motion and in some cases the spine may penetrate to a depth of several inches. At the instant of injury a burst of pain begins to radiate from the point of impact and increases in intensity. The spine is loosely attached to the ray's tail and frequently remains imbedded in the victim's flesh.

Stingray spine.

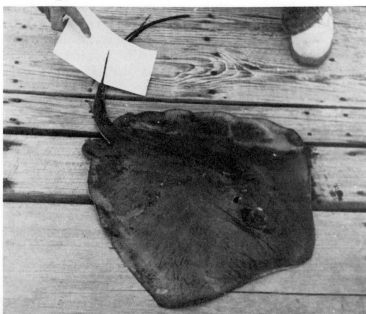

The ray is only temporarily impaired by the loss, since a replacement spine is usually hidden in the flesh of the tail immediately beneath the exposed one. Occasionally two and even three spines may be exposed in a cluster at the same time. This rapid replacement is much like the teeth of a shark, with a new one ready to replace one that has been broken out or become loose.

The degree of severity of a stingray wound is governed by several factors. For some unexplainable reason, certain people seem to possess considerably more tolerance to the venom than others in apparently similar physical condition. Also, the degree of toxicity of the venom varies even in rays of the same species. Another aspect to be considered is the location of the wound and, logically, the depth of penetration.

While infrequent, death has occasionally resulted from the wound of a stingray. In any case, it should not be left unattended. It is important to impress upon the victim that the fatality rate is very low. This is important to one suffering intense pain, because the element of morbid apprehension may bring about a condition of shock which may, within itself, prove fatal. There have been accounts of people with an abnormal phobia of snakes having died of shock when bitten only by a harmless type.

If the spine is imbedded in the flesh deeply enough, the recurved barbs will make on-the-scene extraction hazardous and should be avoided by anyone other than a physician. To do so can result only in aggravated tissue damage and increased envenomation. Therefore, no first-aid treatment is recommended in cases of deep penetration.

If, however, the blow has been a glancing one, resulting in laceration, the wound should be thoroughly washed with an antiseptic solution as quickly as possible. If antiseptic is not immediately available, clean salt water is a substitute and its efficacy will be enhanced if it can be heated, but not so hot as to within itself be painful.

Stingrays can be equally dangerous in or out of the water. Commercial fishermen working nets in shallow bays occasionally are injured by one they have unintentionally hauled

Tip of spine.

aboard their boat. A stingray that is restrained in any manner should be handled with utmost caution.

Failure to exercise proper caution was graphically proven to me some years ago when my son was eleven years old. Our home was only a stone's throw from a narrow pier that extended out into the bay. It was a natural attraction for any youngster interested in the water because it provided a place to catch any of a number of inshore fish, it was a good place to tie skiffs, and near the end the water was deep enough for swimming.

On the morning in question my wife and I were awakened shortly after sunrise by loud shouts from our son that left little doubt in our minds that he had encountered some mishap of a serious nature. He was not the type to become overly excited at minor injuries youngsters are frequently involved in.

Dressing hurriedly, I ran outside and immediately determined the cries were coming from the pier. What had happened was quickly obvious when I saw a stingray on the pier and our son clutching one of his bare feet.

He and a young companion who had spent the night with us had, in the manner of young boys, slipped out of bed at dawn and walked down to the pier. About halfway out toward the end they had looked down in the clear water and spotted the outline of a two-foot-wide stingray that had covered itself with mud. Unable to resist the temptation they had hurried back to the house and picked up a long-handled gig with four metal prongs. Our son made a direct hit, spearing the ray squarely across the head. Aware of the possible danger, he had delivered what he considered the coup de grace by clubbing the ray with the handle of an oar as soon as he had hoisted it up on the pier.

Logically the ray should have been thoroughly subdued and, because his friend was a newcomer to the littoral scene, our son was in the process of demonstrating how a person might be injured by stepping on one while wading.

As soon as he placed his foot on the back, the "dead" ray assisted him in his demonstration with what must have been reflex action. Whatever, the spine struck a glancing blow that cut a gash about two inches long on the side of his foot. Hurriedly examining the injury, I noticed it was less than a quarter of an inch deep. Mixed with a slow ooze of blood there was a considerable amount of thick brown slime from the spine.

This spine of the stingray is covered with an integumentary sheath that completely covers the sharp bony sliver and the recurved barbs along the sides. On the underside of the spine are two grooves extending from the base almost to the tip. These shallow grooves contain the bulk of the venom that spreads out into the slimy sheath.

Picking our son up, I carried him back to the house. Because we knew his nature, my wife and I quickly realized the pain was so severe that he was approaching a state of shock. A trip to the nearest hospital would have taken nearly an hour and a hurried phone call disclosed the only doctor nearby was off on a call. We wasted little time debating what should be done and decided to administer what first aid we could without further delay.

To ease the pain he was given a common aspirin tablet, as nothing more satisfactory was available. His complexion had already become pale and he was perspiring profusely. I knew

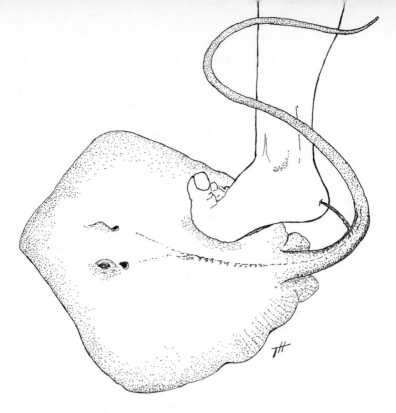

the venom was concentrated in the tiny globs of slime that had become lodged in the wound as the sheath was ruptured. While my wife was preparing a basinful of hot water in which she dissolved about three tablespoonsful of epsom salts, I examined the wound. The area around it had become ashen in color. We immersed his foot in the hot water for about three minutes. The heat of the water caused the wound to begin bleeding more freely and I began the tedious task of removing the fragments of slime with a sterile cotton swab.

At one point, about twenty minutes after the injury occurred, we became quite concerned when we noticed the muscles of his abdomen had become rigid. So much so that pressure with our fingers could not make the flesh yield any more than if we had been pressing on his kneecap. This condition lasted for about fifteen minutes and was followed by several vomiting spells.

With the wound thoroughly cleaned and swabbed with a mild antiseptic, we felt we had exhausted all first-aid measures at our disposal. We decided to make the long trip to the hospital. The ashen color around the wound had changed to bright red and our son was complaining of a dizzy sensation.

While my wife was getting him situated in a prone position on the back seat of the car, I filled a large container with plain tap water and added a considerable amount of ice, putting an extra supply in an insulated ice bucket to be used on the way to the hospital.

After his foot had been in the ice water about five minutes, our son remarked that the pain that had spread up to his hip was beginning to ease. This was some relief, but we were still concerned as to whether or not enough of the venom had been absorbed to bring about a secondary shock that could have serious effects on the cardiovascular system.

The physician in attendance examined him thoroughly and kept him resting in bed for about an hour. During this period his blood pressure and respiration were checked frequently and the doctor assured us he was making a satisfactory recovery. He did, however, administer a tetanus injection to ward off any infection that might develop. The wound was properly bandaged and the only aftereffect we noticed was that our son complained of a dull pain in his foot. This, too, had become so minor as to be ignored by the evening of the following day.

The above might be considered a normal reaction to a moderately severe laceration wound from a stingray spine. Punctures, where the spine is left imbedded in the flesh, are normally more serious.

Because the human constitution varies so much from one person to the next, there can be no exact statement of how many symptoms will be manifested, nor how severe the reaction to each, or all, will be. I once knew an old commercial fisherman who lived an almost hermitlike life on an island on the west coast of Florida. He earned his meager livelihood using a gill net with which he caught enough mullet and other fish to sell to the fish house in the town across the bay.

When I first met him I was immediately curious about the appearance of his feet and lower legs. They were scarred with several dozen deep craters ranging in diameter from the size of a dime to that of a quarter. My first thought was that he must have at one time had a severe case of smallpox. I quickly ruled this out when I noticed that many were very old scars, while others seemed to be of fairly recent origin.

It was not until I had visited him several times that I felt comfortable in asking about the scars. He shifted his battered old pipe from one side of his mouth to the other and rested an ankle on his knee. Examining the indentations with a gnarled thumb, he said: "It's them damned old stingarees," using the southern colloquial term, " 'Peers as if them slick, flat devils is been after me fer back as I can recollect. Used to be they was downright worrisome, 'til I learnt how to deal with 'em."

My interest was whetted and since he seemed quite willing to discuss his injuries, I asked him to explain the treatment he used. "If one jest cuts me," he said, "I don't even mess with it no mo. When I gits stung bad, like when the stinger goes in plum deep, I jest leave it be 'til I gits through wadin' 'round pickin' the fish outa the mesh. Then I biles me a can of salt water an' gits to work with a pair of pliers."

His explanation of his medical approach to the situation was as rustic and tough as the old man himself. It consisted of pouring a dribble of scalding water on the puncture point as he extracted the spine with the pliers.

I discreetly kept my thoughts to myself, but I simply could not believe any human could deliberately inflict such torture on themselves. I remained convinced that he was just spinning a fanciful yarn until one afternoon in the latter part of the summer when I happened to stop by for one of my occasional visits. I had learned to take many of his tales with a grain of salt, but I always enjoyed spending time with him and listening to him tell some of his stories that reached back over nearly seventy-five years.

On this visit he had dragged his net into the shallows and was collecting the remaining fish when I arrived. When he saw me he waved and finished tossing the gilled fish into an open skiff. When he was through he beached the skiff and I noticed as he walked up the beach he was limping.

"Reckon I was 'bout due," he said, looking down at his left

foot. A stingray spine protruded from the fleshy part of his heel. "If you're a mind to, you'd favor me by settin' a fire goin' over yonder under my grill an' git a can o' water bilin'."

In the half hour that followed I stood by and observed in suppressed horror as he performed his crude surgery. Throughout the operation he would pause occasionally to re-heat the water. There was no conversation, but he voiced an outstandingly varied repertoire of epithets that constituted some of the most expressive cursing I have ever heard.

Just as he had previously explained, he slowly poured the water, that was just a degree or two below the boiling point, over the spine, working it out gradually by twisting and pull-ing with the pliers. The venom itself must have been caus-ing intense pain, but I wondered if it was worse than the scalding water.

When the grisly task was done he casually tossed the spine into the fire and lit his pipe. When he had rested he was going to row across the bay with his boatload of fish and was in somewhat of a hurry to get started before the fish house closed for the day. I insisted that I be allowed to tow his boat back and return the following day with his skiff and his money. He agreed with some reluctance, remarking: " 'Twill give me some spare time to mend a few holes I been aimin' to git at in my net."

Prevention is decidedly easier than any form of treatment where stingray injuries are concerned. For the wading angler and the surf bather, the best way to prevent an unpleasant encounter is relatively simple. Because they are not aggres-sive, stingrays are quick to retreat if they have warning. The best way to flush them out of the sand is to slide the feet along the bottom, rather than taking deliberate steps.

Unlike some dangerous creatures that will shy away from areas where people are swimming, the stingray will occa-sionally cruise right in when there are several dozen people in the water. For some reason certain summers seem to be more hazardous than others and at such times numerous people are injured. Then again, still for some unexplained reason, the next summer and the one that follows may pass with stingray injuries being a rarity.

Devilfish and Mantas

Quite often a particular sea creature will gain a completely undeserved reputation of being a threat to mankind. Frequently, just an evil-sounding name is responsible. Again, it may be the result of a fearsome appearance. If a suggestive name is combined with sinister shape and great size, folklore has generally woven numerous tales of horror around such a creature.

The two large mantas, the Atlantic, *Manta birostris,* and the Pacific, *Manta hamiltoni,* are outstanding examples. The real oddity where these two giants are concerned is that they have received their reputation from a lesser ray, popularly known as the devilfish. More properly it is the devil ray, *Mobula hypostoma.* While the devil ray itself is quite large, it is a pygmy compared to the two seagoing behemoths mentioned above.

Not bothering to investigate the difference, there are those who will call either the Atlantic or Pacific mantas "giant devilfish." Up to a point it is an understandable mistake, since all three do look much alike in general appearance. It is what lies beyond this stage that fiction and fact begin to merge and they do so in such a manner as to leave the folklorist wondering just where truth ends and fantasy begins.

There can be little doubt that when the early voyagers first saw the devil ray or the manta they had good reason to apply the name of devilfish. All three unquestionably possess a diabolical countenance seemingly designed to inspire fear. The true devil ray, like the mantas of both oceans, are broad diamond-shaped disks that terminate on either side in what appears to be giant wings. They are, like the wings of the smaller rays, enlarged pectoral fins and they constitute the major surface area of the creature's body. The wings begin at the heads, taper to pointed tips and then slope back at approximately the same angle to the base of the tail.

On each side of the head there are long fleshy appendages known as cephalic fins that resemble horns. They are in reality modified arms that are used to sweep food into the ray's mouth. The true devil ray grows to about four feet from one side to the other with a whiplike tail at the posterior end. The color is dull black on top and yellowish white below.

They are primarily bottom feeders and differ from the mantas in that the mouth is located just beneath the head. In shallow water they will frequently be observed moving along the bottom as they feed on crustaceans and small school fish. When startled by the approach of a boat they will put on a burst of speed that sends them ahead swiftly. Also like the mantas, they will occasionally zoom to the surface and erupt in a jump that will carry them several feet into the air.

Both the Atlantic and Pacific mantas closely resemble one another in general shape and size. They differ from the devil ray and several other closely related species of large rays, in that the wide mouth is situated at the front of the head. This, too, is flanked by cephalic, or head fins, and used to sweep food into the mouth.

Adult mantas may reach a width of over twenty feet with large eyes positioned on each side of the head. They have whiplike tails, with those of the Atlantic variety being considerably longer than their Pacific cousins. They are occasionally seen cruising close to the surface and at times will rest motionless on the bottom for short periods.

Atlantic manta, swimming.

The weight of a full-grown Atlantic manta has been recorded at nearly two tons, which is almost twice the weight of those found in the eastern Pacific. For a creature so large and with such a wide mouth, it is difficult to believe they would be content to feed only on such food as shrimp, small school fish, and even plankton. Such is the case, however, and the tooth structure alone suggests that larger creatures are never eaten. The teeth are in the form of flattened grinders near the throat and are suitable only for mashing the small fish life before it is swallowed.

There is a minor difference in the color of these two large species. Younger specimens of the Atlantic manta are basically black with a faint hue of reddish brown or green providing the only color. As they grow older all tinge of color vanishes and the entire dorsal surface is dull black. The Pacific manta is much the same with the exception of two distinct stripes of yellowish white which begin on each side of the head, angling back to form a large V that comes to a point near the center of the back. Both species are dull white underneath.

There are two interesting facts concerning the birth of mantas. One is that the eggs are hatched internally and the young are born alive. This ovoviviparity is not uncommon in other forms of life, but the oddity comes in the manner in which the young mantas are introduced into the world. It may not always occur in such a spectacular manner, but it is the way it has been most frequently observed.

Groups of mantas that may number only three or four, or as many as several dozen, may enter a bay and suddenly commence to hurl themselves into the air. Countless observers have witnessed the sudden aerial birth of a young manta while the female is in the air. It is not known if such births are normal, or the premature birth of young that were about to be born. One way or the other, the young mantas seem to suffer no ill effects and begin swimming in a normal manner. Those produced by a fully developed female measure about four feet in width and weigh well over twenty-five pounds.

One question that is often asked is whether or not the jumping is restricted to the females. It is believed that both

Manta (Pacific) in jump.

sexes jump, but no one knows for sure just why. Some fish jump when they are being pursued by predators, others when they are suddenly startled, while still others seemingly jump simply because they want to. The most popular theory concerning the spectacular leaps of mantas is that they are trying to dislodge parasites or remoras. The remoras do no harm to their host unless it is to impede swimming when too many collect on a single manta.

Mantas do occasionally jump while swimming in open water, but they seem to indulge in the practice much more frequently when they have entered a bay. Despite the reason, it is interesting to speculate on the speed a two-ton manta must be forced to generate in order to hurl its huge bulk well clear of the surface. Their normal swimming speed is quite slow compared to many true fish, but it is known they can move swiftly when they feel called upon to do so. It may be that their flattened body, with its kitelike shape, is of decided assistance when they want to jump.

One of the most illogical, yet widespread, horror stories concerning these creatures is that they will attack a swimmer and press him to the bottom, holding him there until he drowns. Equally absurd is another belief that they will cruise

Very young manta with remoras attached.

along beside a human and administer a severe lashing with their long rough tails. Lacking any dependable accounts of such happenings, it must be assumed that both stories are composed of imagination.

More credible, but still uncommon, are the stories of mantas either upsetting or crashing down on a small boat when a school of them go on a jumping spree. Almost anyone who has spent considerable time in a small boat in southern waters has been startled almost out of their wits when the jumping and somersaulting begins nearby.

To watch such action during the daylight hours is an interesting show. To hear their massive bodies landing flat on the surface at night is something entirely different. The sudden blasts of sound can be likened to cannon fire. If one happens to make a jump close to a boat it can be somewhat unnerving to the occupants. One has only to imagine what the outcome would be to have a couple of tons of solid flesh crashing down on them. Even to be grazed by the tip of one of the giant's wings could be disastrous to a small boat and those aboard.

In all probability, if such did occur, it would be completely by accident, since the impact would, in all likelihood, severely injure the manta. Just being aware that many fish will occasionally become confused and jump toward a light makes the nocturnal boater apprehensive when he hears the activity somewhere off in the darkness.

One unsettling stunt mantas will perform from time to time that has occurred and been documented is that of taking an anchored boat off on an unplanned ride. A cruising manta will, either by intent or accident, grasp the anchor or anchor line and tow the attached boat around for several minutes.

In all probability, what happens is that the manta sweeps beneath the boat, runs afoul the anchor line, dislodges the anchor from the bottom, and continues swimming. If the line is between the two cephalic fins the steady pull will draw the anchor up until it becomes caught in the manta's broad mouth. Quite logically, this causes it to become excited and, in an effort to rid itself of the bothersome object, begins to swim faster and dart from side to side. All the while the bewildered fishermen cling to any convenient handholds and wonder why they ever decided to go fishing in the first place.

As a rule, unless one of the boat's occupants has the presence of mind to slash the line with his knife, the manta continues taking the boaters on a Nantucket sleighride. Eventually it will find a way to get the anchor free of its mouth and, often as not, erupts in a jump to celebrate his victory.

Mantas are frequently harpooned by commercial fishermen suitably rigged to handle their catch. When they are caught on a commercial basis the hides of some are used as an abrasive in cabinetwork the same as shark skin. Most of the flesh is sold for fish meal and the large livers are valuable for the oil they contain. Parts of the flesh are occasionally cut into fillets and sold as fish under a variety of names.

Sawfish

When I was about five years old there was quite a stir in the small Florida town on the Gulf where I lived. A group of commercial fishermen had captured a "sea monster" and strung the creature up to a gin pole on the boat dock. The word spread rapidly and in due course I was taken down to the waterfront to stare in wide-eyed wonder at the fantastic catch.

No one thought of charging admission, nor was there an entrepreneur on hand with a straw hat and cane to give a spiel about the creature that had been dredged up from the depths. It was just a big oddity to be viewed and discussed by those who might be interested.

There, in touching distance if I had dared, I beheld the monster. Someone had measured and it was common knowledge that the creature was seventeen feet long. I was told it was a sawfish—although there were some who mistakenly called it a swordfish. If you stood around and listened there were all manner of tales to be heard about the giant that dangled from a heavy line that had been tied around its tail.

Some, who seemed devoid of imagination, casually remarked on how they wished many more could be caught because they ate entirely too many oysters and crabs. I found it more fascinating to listen to others who related wild tales they had heard about how large sawfish would attack boats, saw them in half, and proceed to butcher the human occupants. Still others told how such beasts were known to invade swimming beaches and cut the feet off any and all who failed to get out of the water in time.

One thing was certain: No one was going to make me believe that such a fearful-looking brute would be content to dine on oysters and crabs. The longer I gazed in wide-eyed

Sawfish hanging from gin pole.

wonder the more convinced I became that this thing they called a sawfish was undoubtedly the most dangerous creature the sea had to offer.

From time to time I had been taken down to the waterfront to see extra large sharks that had also been placed on public display. Their bulk and ragged teeth protruding from a gaping mouth had been a source of wonder, but pilloried dead sharks seemed commonplace in comparison with this giant I now beheld. Long pointed teeth, so many that I could not pretend to count them, jutted at right angles from a broad flat snout protruding from the front of the creature's head. It resembled a section of a crosscut saw with teeth on both sides of the blade.

Feed on oysters and crabs, indeed!

The years passed and my interest in sea life continued with fishing, observing, collecting, studying, and wondering, but the memory of that seventeen-foot sawfish has never dimmed. In the early years I simply could not accept the fact that nature would build such a magnificent living weapon of destruction and then decree that it should use that awesome saw to grub about in the bottom mud uprooting bivalves and flushing out crabs. It seemed tantamount to sending a knight in shining armor out to dig potatoes, when he should be busy slaying fire-breathing dragons.

There are two primary species of these strange creatures in the western Atlantic and nine recognized species in the genus Pristis distributed around the world in tropical, subtropical, and some temperate zone waters. One of the most numerous is the common sawfish, *Pristis pectinatus*, ranging from New York southward.

The real giant of the clan is the largetooth sawfish, *Pristis perotteti*, known to reach a length of twenty feet and exceed a thousand pounds in weight. All are members of the order Rajiformes, which includes the rays and skates and, in turn, makes them relatives of the sharks.

Like most others of its kind, the largetooth sawfish spends much of the time in relatively shallow water close to the coast. It is not uncommon to find them exploring the brackish waters of tropical and subtropical rivers. Generally, they plod

Sawfish, swimming.

along at an unhurried pace, stirring up the bottom ooze with
their saw, forever in search of crabs and other forms of sea
life that require little or no speed or agility to capture. Occasionally, when a school of mullet or similar fish passes
nearby, the sawfish will seemingly be roused from its lethargy
long enough to slash about in the school. When it has killed
and wounded a sufficient number it will return to the bottom
and leisurely collect whatever has not already been stolen by
more active fish that may be nearby.

They mate like sharks and rays and the young are born
alive, entering the watery world as miniature copies of their
parents, including the tooth-studded saw. To answer the inevitable question . . . At the time of birth the saws are covered with a protective sheath, but it quickly wears away as
they begin rooting about the bottom in search of food.

They are powerful fish and when one of moderate size is
trapped in a seine or net they can cause considerable damage
to the mesh in their bid for freedom. Frequenting shallow
coastal waters they could be a serious threat to swimmers and
wading fishermen. Generally, however, they prefer to swim
away without causing any disturbance. Unlike stingrays, they
do not conceal themselves under sand or mud so that they
would pose a threat if they were accidentally stepped on. Because of their mouth and tooth structure they could not make
use of any large creature they might kill.

People have been injured by them, and sometimes severely so, but most often this has happened as a result of

247

careless handling of one that has been trapped in a net. Other incidences have occurred when they have been hooked and brought alongside a boat without observing the necessary precautions for handling a potentially dangerous creature.

During my travels through the West Indies I heard several accounts of conflict between humans and large sawfish that were too realistically reported to have been composed of whole cloth. One involved two newcomers to the tropics who worked for United Fruit Company in Honduras. After a full week of supervising the loading of countless tons of bananas, the two men enjoyed getting out on the bay near Puerto Cortés and experimenting with the abundant and varied forms of fishing that were immediately available.

Their craft was a seventeen-foot catboat and on the day they encountered their sawfish they were about a quarter mile from shore trying to hook a shark. Shortly after letting a hook baited with a whole fish sink to the bottom they saw the stout handline being rapidly pulled over the stern. After a considerable struggle the fishermen were able to see their catch. It had the body of a shark, but they had never heard of a shark with a long tooth-studded snout.

Along with their fishing tackle they had included a heavy revolver. When they had struggled with their catch, which they estimated to have been at least twelve feet in length, they shot it several times. The lead slugs seemed to have had the desired effect and, since their strange catch was showing no signs of life, they went about the task of hauling it aboard. Their objective was to return it to town and see if anyone could identify the creature—or maybe confirm their suspicion that they had hooked something no one had ever seen before.

About halfway back one of the men decided to examine the catch more extensively. He attempted to roll it over and just at that moment the sawfish *came back to life.*

In a matter of several minutes packed with explosive action the sawfish severely gashed the legs of one of the tyro fishermen and the other was knocked overboard. The sawfish, bullet-ridden as it was, continued its bid for escape and did not stop until it had splintered one side of the boat and made its way back into the water.

Battered and bleeding, the two men clung onto what was left of their catboat. They shifted their weight to the undamaged side and bailed as fast as they were able to keep ahead of the water that flowed through the broken planking. Eventually they were rescued by a bumboat and returned to Puerto Cortés.

After they were released from the local medical dispensary with numerous stitches and bandages, they related their story. Local inhabitants told them what they had caught and admonished them never to try to boat a large sawfish again, even though it appeared to be dead. It was a warning neither fisherman needed.

While in the same area I repeatedly heard a story from a number of different sources. The accounts were remarkably consistent, which is a reasonably fair test of truthfulness, but it still must be related as an "as-told" story. If, by chance, it is true, it could be listed as an unprovoked attack by a sawfish that ended in a fatality.

It also occurred at Puerto Cortés and involved a fifteen-year-old native boy who had been present when a lighter was being unloaded at a low pier on the waterfront. During the operation a case of canned goods fell from the cargo net and broke open when it hit a piling, spilling the cans into the water. To the boy, who was an excellent swimmer, the cans of food represented little short of a real treasure. When he learned the owners had no intentions of salvaging the cans, he enlisted the aid of his brother to guard the cans as he dived again and again to bring them up and toss them up on the pier.

The water was exceptionally clear and several local fishermen and those who frequented the waterfront stood around watching the active youngster. It was not uncommon for large sawfish to forage about under the wharfs and piers. When some of the bystanders noticed one with a saw "over four feet long" they waited until the boy surfaced and casually told him of the creature's presence. If the warning had been of a large shark or barracuda, the boy would have almost certainly scrambled for safety, but he chose to let the sawfish warning go unheeded.

Much to everyone's surprise, the large sawfish made a sudden rush toward the diver and slashed him across the abdomen. The injury was so severe that those on the dock could see the youngster's intestines had spilled out and he was thrashing about in a cloud of bloody water. If the sawfish had left the scene immediately it is likely someone would have attempted a rescue, but it continued to circle about, seemingly intrigued with the shiny cans.

By the time the creature became disinterested and moved on, the boy was dead, probably from a combination of drowning and loss of blood. Assuming the story is basically true, it is possible that the sawfish was attracted by the flash of the tin cans and its dull brain may have told it the boy was just another fish that was robbing it of a potential meal.

Since that day when I saw my first sawfish I have fished for them at numerous places around the world. They can put up a protracted struggle at the end of a line, but it is doubtful that anyone would ever suggest they be classed as game fish. Despite their potential danger from a combination of their muscular body and frightful saw, they cause little trouble if unmolested.

Why nature armed it with such a weapon and then decreed that it should rummage about the bottom for its food is a mystery that can never be solved.

9

Killer Whales

The killer whale, *Orcinus orca*, are members of the suborder, Odontoceti, which includes the toothed whales and certain members of the porpoise and dolphin group. They are found in all oceans from pole to pole. Even one of moderate size would be capable of swallowing a man and still have the appetite and stomach capacity for devouring several more.

Unlike sharks that are known to occasionally maim, kill, and eat humans, there are no authenticated cases to prove the orca, as the killer whale is often known, has ever included man in its diet. Dependable eye-witness accounts and scientific examination of their stomach contents prove their appetite is as varied as it is prodigious. Fish, squid, porpoise, and seals rate high on their diet.

As an example of their enormous appetite, one specimen was found to have swallowed thirteen porpoises and fourteen seals. Still another was killed and when its stomach was opened it was found to contain the remains of thirty-two adult seals that had been recently eaten. Whalers, virtually the only sea hunters capable of subduing an adult orca, have testified to finding human remains in their stomachs. Such reports are spotty and reach back over many years of seafaring. The dependability of such reports is naturally open to question, but when their known diet is considered, it is doubtful there would be any reason they would exclude a human if the opportunity presented itself. The few individual

Killer whale in full jump.

specimens in aquariums that provide spectacular entertainment as they cavort with their keepers cannot be considered. They are, after all, captives existing under conditions entirely different from those that roam the sea at will.

Like their close relatives, the whales and porpoise, they are true mammals. They must surface frequently for a breath of air and if prevented from doing so will drown. They give birth to their young alive, suckle, and protect them from would-be predators. They travel in pods or packs. The choice of the term depends on the conditions under which the human observer views a collection of them. If, for example, they are viewed from the safety of a ship's deck or a vantage point along the coast, and if the group of orcas is traveling peacefully along, they are likely to be referred to as a pod. On the other hand, if they are observed killing a giant whale or engaged in rampant slaughter of numerous swimming seals, the term "pack" will seem more appropriate.

They apparently are family-oriented and are usually spotted in groups of ten or fifteen, although there may be as many as three dozen traveling together. It is strongly suspected that the largest and strongest bull is the leader. The large males are readily distinguishable from the cows because of the predominantly higher dorsal fin.

When hunting, the size of their prey does not seem to enter

the picture. They may be surging about in a school of salmon or attacking a huge blue whale fifteen or twenty times their size. To see them engaged in this orgy is to witness one of the most savage encounters in all of nature. The hapless whale is set upon on all sides and the killers engage in a true bloodbath. Their pattern of attack is to concentrate on tearing the whales' huge pectoral fins and flukes to shreds, while others are ripping away at the monster's mouth. As the whale becomes weakened and incapacitated, the pack begins to bite large chunks of flesh from the dying body.

There are times when their ferocity seems unbounded and their ability to assay a situation and apply uncanny logic staggers the human imagination. Robert Scott's last Antarctic expedition in 1911 is a good example and one which was photographically recorded.

A pack of orcas spotted the explorers and their sled dogs on ice floes. In an effort to get at them they first attempted to hurl their bodies up on the ice. Sensing that the explorers were huddling near the centers of the ice rafts, the killers began breaking the floes by plunging against the bottom of the thinner edges. By good fortune the men were able to move to safer ice before any were lost. It did prove, however, that the pack of orcas had begun working as a team to accomplish their objective.

This was not some wild tale fabricated by sailors with vivid imaginations, but part of a scientific report, backed by photographic proof. Not only does it demonstrate a display of logic, but it is a testimony of the brute strength possessed by these creatures.

Despite their ferociousness, the killer whales are beautiful creatures that seem to be dressed for a night at the opera. The majority of their body is jet black, with a snow white chin and underside. There is a large white patch just above the eye and a larger snowy spot farther back along the side.

The eyes are set back on the sides of the head, but in such a position that they can see ahead, as well as to the side. This ability is unique in the whale clan, with many of the others able to see only off to each side, thus precluding any sense of depth perception.

Both top and bottom jaws are studded with large conical teeth which interlock when the mouth is shut. They have one large dorsal fin located near the center of the back. On a full-grown male this fin bends backward at the tip and it has been suggested that untrained observers have mistaken it as part of some unknown sea monster. In examining a photograph of the fin alone, it requires little imagination to see some creature with a long, thick neck and small head cruising along through the waves.

As with the porpoise and other whales, the orca's anatomy poses a question that provides material for interesting speculation. The skeleton shows distinct vestigial hip bones that suggest, once in the dim past, they had hind legs. Added to this are the five handlike bones in each of the two pectoral fins. Today they serve to strengthen these flippers, but once they could have been the front feet of the creature.

There can be no positive answer, but one cannot help wondering if these animals once plodded about on land and eventually returned to the sea. Perhaps they came from the sea, tried terrestrial life for an aeon or two, and gradually readapted their structure as they returned to the region of their origin.

For an animal so large, the orca can surface, replenish its supply of air, and submerge with remarkable speed. If it has urgent business below it can break the surface, exhale the stale air in its lungs, and replace it in a single second. Under normal conditions they do this every minute or two, but if the situation warrants it, they can stay submerged for more than ten minutes.

This breathing operation is accomplished, as with other members of the clan, through a blowhole located on the top of the head. The valve that controls the opening and closing is so sensitive that it will close instantly unless the blowhole is in the air, thereby preventing the intake of water into the lungs should a wave wash over the head.

When an orca is born it emerges tail first into its watery world. This is of distinct importance, because once its head is clear of the mother's body it must be boosted quickly to the surface so that it may draw its first breath of air. The size of an average infant will measure seven feet in length at birth. It is capable of swimming immediately, but should the orca experience difficulty it will receive assistance from its mother and other females in the pod.

Until it has gained weight and strength it depends on its mother to supply milk. This seemingly impossible task is accomplished with nearly the speed of breathing. The young simply nudges the mother at an aperture on the underside near the tail. The shape of its mouth and lacking flexible lips make conventional nursing out of the question. Instead, it opens its mouth at the instant of nudging and the female discharges a jet of rich milk into the infant's throat.

Prodigious amounts of study and experimentation have been conducted to unravel the mystery of porpoise, including orca, speech. It has been well established that they do communicate with one another and many investigators believe they even have the equivalent of a language. It seems certain that the strange noises are not just cries of alarm or the desire for companionship. The sounds one hears when observing these creatures at oceanariums is only an insignificant group of sounds. The true "talk" has been recorded and found to cover an extensive range, much of which is inaudible to the human ear.

So refined is their echolocation apparatus that it makes man's sophisticated electronic equipment comparable to some device hatched up by children playing with empty cans and a strand of copper wire. All of these mammals emit a series of high-speed "clicks" that travel through the water and bounce off any obstruction. The echo then returns and the highly developed brain considers the lapse of time and direction and computes all pertinent data in a fraction of a second. Not only are they constantly aware of the depth of water through which they are swimming but also what lies ahead, as well as the location of other members.

This skill is so highly developed that captive specimens can tell in an instant whether or not an object tossed in the water is something they would like or just a substitute man has used to test their ability. They can, for example, recognize immediately if a fish is one they would normally eat, or whether it is one of the same size, but of a type they consider a poor substitute.

Of course, these and other findings are the result of work done with captives in tanks and holding pens. While such experiments have contributed enormously to man's store of knowledge, it is almost certain to have only scratched the surface. What additional skills they may possess and utilize when unrestricted is unknown.

The orca, like the porpoise that have come under scientific scrutiny, are known to have very large brains. Scientists have generally agreed that the size of the brain is not necessarily proof of superior intelligence if the difference in size is relatively minor. It cannot be denied, however, that few creatures are capable of such swift learning, as well as the ability to remember and use reason before acting.

A few orcas had been captured and held for short periods before they died from time to time over the years. Not until 1965 was a healthy and uninjured specimen successfully maintained in captivity for a long enough period to afford extensive study. The man responsible for this is Edward I. Griffin, owner and director of the Seattle Public Aquarium.

The orca, which Griffin named Namu, was trapped in a salmon net in the waters off British Columbia near the town of Namu. The killer whale was a twenty-four-footer weighing approximately five tons. Griffin not only engineered the Herculean task of transporting his captive over a distance of 450 miles from Fitz Hugh Sound, British Columbia, to the Seattle aquarium on Puget Sound but he set about the treacherous process of making friends with the huge killer. Since then others have been captured and are maintained at a few oceanariums and the close study of these has been extensive. Not only have some established beliefs been proven and others disproven but the scientific store of knowledge is continuing to grow with each passing day.

Are killer whales as dangerous and ferocious as previously believed? The answer is basically yes, and perhaps even more so. In light of the behavior of some captives, however, the positive answer must necessarily be tempered with the added statement that individual specimens undoubtedly have different personalities. It would seem that, in some respects, they are much like tigers, lions, and other large animals. Some will accept captivity and display affection for their keepers, while others rebel with violence.

If people can safely get into aquariums with these great killers, is it not then reasonable to say those out of captivity would never harm a human swimmer? The difference in surroundings is too extensive to be used as an accurate yardstick. Men and women regularly go into cages with tigers and lions. At the same time people are killed by these cats in the wild—and occasionally in cages.

It has been said that man is not part of the normal diet of the orca. For that matter, neither is the human a regular part of the diet of sharks. If called upon to prepare a list of creatures that comprise the normal diet of a tiger, no reasonable zoologist would include humans. Logically, much depends on the situation at the moment and the attitude of the individual animal in question. However, for a beast that is known to have eaten thirty-two full grown seals in a single feeding spree, the act of sampling one human seems to speak for itself.

10

Red Tide

The red tide. Just the words are enough to cause areas that are largely dependent upon tourist trade to wish their natural attractions were ski slopes or another Grand Canyon. The state of Florida, and particularly its Gulf Coast, is doubtlessly the one section of North America that dreads the red tide the most. The reason is that of all the state's natural and man-made attractions, the sparkling sunlit beaches are the greatest drawing card for tourists, and these beaches are the most severely affected when the red tide goes into action.

The red tide is not restricted entirely to the west coast of Florida. There is, however, no question that this is the state and, for that matter, part of the world that receives the most extensive and adverse publicity when nature decides to put on one of its offensive shows. Certainly the red tide does not rival massive earthquakes, exploding volcanos, or even a rash of killer tornados, but from a standpoint of financial loss of serious proportions it touches thousands of people per coastal mile.

When an overbloom is in progress it sends a few people to the hospital, many more are made moderately ill, tourists cancel reservations, real estate takes a nosedive, and permanent residents grouse about the lingering and evil smell that hangs heavy in the air. Of considerably more importance, fish are killed, not just by the thousands, but by the thousands of tons. All of this by a creature so small that over seventy million can exist in a single bucket of water, and a small bucket at that!

The red tide has marine scientists baffled on several important counts. They know *what* it is, but they do not know what causes it to suddenly react in an adverse manner. They cannot predict it and they can find no suitable way to stop it once it has begun.

Some years ago when the civilized world was becoming increasingly concerned with man-made pollution of air, land, and water there was a loud hue and cry by those who believed the red tide was the direct result of the wanton discharge of human, agricultural, and factory wastes that flowed into the Gulf.

It would almost have been a blessing if this were so. If it were so it would have been a potent weapon in the hands of those interested in preventing the human race from destroying itself by pollution. Heedless as man may be of fouling his environment, there is no clear-cut evidence to prove that he is responsible for the red tide.

It seems, instead, to be a destructive phenomenon created solely by nature. Reports of outbreaks date well back into history, and one of the best documented reports was penned in 1884 by an observer named S. T. Walker. It had been only thirty-three years earlier that Dr. John Gorrie had patented the process for the artificial manufacture of ice. Plants to produce it were costly and commercial fishermen along the west coast of Florida could ill afford the expense. To prevent spoilage of their catch on extended trips the fishermen used large tanks through which clean seawater could flow. It was a primitive method, but without ice it was the only practical solution.

Naturally, Walker had no idea what caused the red tide and, for that matter, he did not even know what it was. He did observe that some of the fishing vessels could make the return trip with the catch in good condition. Others, he reported, had the misfortune of sailing through streaks of "poisoned water" and all of the fish they had caught died in the tanks. Of course, people lived along Florida's west coast at the time, but it was to be a very long time before any kind

Lone angler on clean beach.

Fish-littered beach.

Man cleaning dead fish from beach.

of man-made pollution became a problem in that section of the country.

Some historians believe the same red tide phenomenon we know today is mentioned in Exodus, chapter 7, verses 20 and 21: ". . . and all the waters that were in the river were turned to blood and the fish that was in the river died; and the river stank, and the Egyptians could not drink of the water of the river; and there was blood throughout all the land of Egypt . . ."

The decision as to whether or not the reference concerns the red tide must be a theological opinion. While the description aptly describes a severe overbloom, the red tide as we know it today is primarily restricted to salt water. Outbreaks are, however, worldwide in occurrence with the waters of India, Japan, Africa, southern California, and both coasts of South America being most often affected.

It was not until 1948 that the true villain of the red tide was discovered. It is a microorganism known as *Gymnodinium breve*. It is called a naked dinoflagellate, with the word naked meaning that it has no shell or armor, as have some related species. It is divided into four quadrants on the ventral side. Reproduction is by division, with one becoming two and each new organism maturing swiftly.

It is interesting to note that no ingested food has been isolated, suggesting that it is quasi-holophytic—obtaining its sustenance in the manner of green plants. It survives in nutrient-poor water, but is autotrophic and requires intervals of sunlight for survival.

Like all living things, it must have some form of food and because of its autotrophic nature, carbonates and inorganic nitrogen are the main source, with phosphorus and trace metals probably serving to feed it and encourage growth. *G. breve* is always present in seawater, and on the Gulf Coast of Florida, for example, it seems content to maintain an inoffensive level for anywhere from a year to several years.

Then, for some unexplained reason, it suddenly experiences a population explosion of astronomical proportions. If, in doing so, the swiftly multiplying organisms are moved

Red tide in California waters.

shoreward by prolonged winds and steady currents the affected region begins to experience a "red tide."

The name is frequently misleading, since the color of the water may vary from dull red to brown to chalky green. A dramatic demonstration of what it does to clean seawater can be demonstrated by bringing up a container of the contaminated water and allowing it to stand for a few minutes. Then, when a hand is dipped into the container it is immediately noticeable that the water has developed a viscidity similar to diluted syrup.

In open water it is not necessary for the concentration to be this thick and slimy and to be lethal to all forms of sea life that depend on some form of gills. A moderate outbreak, when the count of *G. breve* is three or four million cells in a quart of water, can destroy tons of fish life. Such a count has on occasions skyrocketed to 75 million cells in the same amount of water. A count as low as a quarter of a million per quart begins to kill fish life.

If for a moment one could draw on his imagination and cast himself in the role of a fish, the scene below the surface would resemble something from a horror movie dealing with some strange nerve gas as a weapon of war.

In the sea just day-to-day living for most forms of life is a junglelike existence where the law of the survival of the fittest is the rule. Suddenly, like some insidious and invisible plague, the world begins to change.

Breathing becomes strangely difficult and the fish cannot help but notice that others of its species are beginning to act in an unnatural manner. The law of the jungle slows down. Gone is the desire to chase normal prey. All the way up and down the scale of life an undeclared truce seems to have gone into effect. Steadily the environment becomes increasingly foul. The predator ceases to chase and the prey runs headlong into its enemy and makes no effort to escape because no danger of being eaten exists.

Tight-knit schools disburse. Some dart about frantically, diving for the safety of the bottom, find it just as bad and race for the surface, but it is no better there. Some swim shoreward, or head for open sea. Large fish and little ones behave in a highly abnormal manner. All around are those swimming on their sides, upside down, or tilted in a vertical position. Crabs on the bottom are floating with the current and shellfish have relaxed so that their flesh is exposed. A force nature has not taught them to deal with is becoming increasingly deadly. The unseen dinoflagellate count is out of control and clouds of lethal water continue to mushroom in size.

Whether the count is low or high, the method by which *G. breve* kills is the same. It contains a poison that is of a neurotoxic nature. When the fish swims into the concentration the poison causes a paralysis of the gills. The resulting oxygen deprivation manifests itself by a loss of balance and erratic gasping, much the same as it would if the same fish were tossed in the bottom of a boat or pulled up on the beach. Depending on the type of fish, as well as the concen-

Typical red tide scene on Florida's west coast.

tration of the organisms in the water, the time required for death may vary from a few minutes to several hours. Despite the time, death by a combination of suffocation and poisoning is the ultimate goal unless, by sheer luck, the fish manages to break through the cloud into open water and swim away from its unseen peril.

Shellfish and many slow-moving bottom fish are frequently the first to become contaminated and it is through them that humans are likely to become seriously poisoned. This is especially true if people eat the shellfish before the health authorities can broadcast sufficient warnings.

Even the shark, capable of withstanding punishment that would kill true fish almost immediately, will die if the concentration becomes too intense. In the prolonged overbloom that continued from the beginning of 1974 and lasted well into the summer, the Mote Marine Laboratory south of Tampa Bay lost all of its sharks. They were being kept in holding pens and tanks and used for study. When the tide of contaminated water began to flow into these areas the sharks fell victim.

Conversely, sharks have been observed swimming through open bay water feeding on the vast windrows of bloated fish carcasses floating on the surface. Since it would be virtually impossible to keep track of free-swimming sharks that indulge in such a diet it is not known what, if any, effects such food would have on their health. Considering the variety of putrid flesh a shark will eat, it is reasonable to assume it is not bothered. They must, however, delay their scavenger work until the concentration of the microorganisms has subsided to a safe level.

The danger to human health as a result of eating contaminated fish is relatively minor. An exception is those who eat shellfish before it is generally known that the red tide is beginning. The problem of eating fish of any kind quickly solves itself, because with the lingering smell of decaying fish in the air, few people are able to maintain an appetite for seafood of any kind. Even commercial concerns that have fish

Cleanup men on Florida beach.

shipped in from other parts of the country find a depressed market.

Scientific investigation has constantly been confounded in its effort to determine the reason this deadly microorganism suddenly begins to multiply into lethal proportions. One popular theory seemed to be dependable and records confirmed it for a number of years. This was that the late summer and early fall were the most red tide prone period of any year. About the time this gained a foothold nature changed the signals and outbreaks began to occur one year in the middle of the winter, or the middle of the spring or early summer. Again, long periods of calm weather, especially when preceded by a season of heavy rainfall, seemed to be a sure indicator. Like other carefully researched theories, this, too, was found undependable.

Some investigators are keeping close check on the change of water temperature in hopes of finding a way to accurately predict when an outbreak can be expected. Others are suspicious of an abnormal flow of freshwater springs that discharge into the Gulf. Numerous chemical attempts at controlling an overbloom have looked promising, only to fail completely or fall far short of expectations when the need has been the most acute.

There is one fact about which those who have done the research are in general agreement. This is, to find the answer of accurately predicting when an outbreak will occur and, hopefully, how to control it is not going to be the result of "crash" programs of short duration. Such has been the practice in the past and, while valuable information has been accumulated each time, the financing has slowed and public concern quickly wanes as the tide subsides. When the trouble starts anew fresh programs are begun, often with different research panels, and much of the previous work is duplicated.

When countless thousands of tons of valuable fish are killed and have to be gathered and buried in a period of a few months the loss is serious. As the shortage of the world food supply becomes increasingly more important, the need for long range and continuing study is more significant.

Mass of fish on beach.

In the final analysis, science may actually conclude that, as offensive and costly as it is, the red tide should not be controlled, even should a positive cure be found. Since it is a natural phenomenon, investigation may disclose there is a good reason why it should occur. This philosophic outlook is not likely to gain widespread acceptance by those in the tourist trade and the people who periodically have to live with the smell. However, it cannot be denied that mankind is repeatedly discovering that tampering with the balance of nature is a treacherous game.

Enthusiasm for sport fishing takes a noticeable nosedive in

popularity during an outbreak of the red tide. The reason is twofold: People simply lose interest in fish because of the constant noxious smell and also, many believe they may be running a risk of developing some illness if they catch and eat fish that have been contaminated. The latter is invalid, since once a fish has been even mildly affected it is going to abstain from feeding. Those fish who do take bait or strike at an artificial lure are as healthy as they would be under normal conditions and present no health hazard.

Those viewing the vast numbers of dead fish for the first time logically conclude that it will be years before the fish population can return to normal. Naturally, fishing luck will be sparse in the immediate wake of a severe kill, but the recovery time is surprisingly fast once the trouble has subsided.

The reason for the speedy recovery of normal fishing conditions in a damaged area is somewhat of a mystery within itself. The general belief is that as soon as the water conditions return to normal, adult fish desert their distant range and move into the void left by the kill to feed on the fry that hatches and other forms of life that simultaneously infiltrate the region. Added to this are the many types of desirable fishes of a migratory nature that are out of the region when the tide occurs.

One of the most perplexing features, however, is that not only is there a fairly rapid recovery of desirable fish but those less desirable such as the sea catfish and stingrays begin to reappear at about the same rate. Because they are relatively slow-moving fish, they are among the first to be killed by the red tide. It can be assumed that others of their kind begin to be drawn by some unknown force toward the empty area.

Fortunately, this microorganism is restricted to relatively small areas. If it should ever become widespread over the oceans of the world it could conceivably put an end to all fish life. Dependent as the human race already is on the vast harvest of fish, such a loss would be catastrophic. If such came to pass and remains as uncontrollable as it is today, infinitesimal *Gymnodinium breve* would be the most dangerous sea creature mankind has ever known.

PHOTO CREDITS

All photographs, unless otherwise credited, are from the author's collection. All drawings were done by the author.

AP Wire Photo: 263
Bahamas News Bureau Photo: 102
From *Dangerous Marine Animals* ("Bolin") by B. W. Halstead, M.D., © 1959, Cornel Maritime Press: 167
Dorden's Photo Studio: 153
Florida Photo, Florida News Bureau, Dept. of Commerce: x, 3, 88, 101, 260 (top)
Burton McNeely: 12
Marineland Studios, Marineland, Florida: 44, 48, 61, 62, 69, 78, 82, 83, 89, 90, 91, 97, 107, 117, 121, 133, 134, 137, 139, 143, 145, 149, 159, 161, 164, 171, 173, 188, 194, 198, 203, 211, 212, 216, 217, 226 (both), 227, 228, 239, 247
Miami Seaquarium, Press Department: 103
Sea World of Florida: 40, 60, 108, 109, 252
Tampa Tribune-Times: 260 (bottom), 261, 265, 266, 268
U.S. Navy Photo: 155, 189
Wide World Photo: 191
Wometco Miami Seaquarium, Jim Latourette: 41, 46, 181, 199 (both), 209, 242

Index

(Page numbers in boldface indicate illustrations.)